Heartfelt Memorial Services

Your Guide for Planning Meaningful Funerals, Celebrations of Life, and Times of Remembrance

Beverly Molander
Dave Savage

Praise for Heartfelt Memorial Services

We are not born into this world with an instruction book on how to live, and neither are we left with one that guides us upon leaving. Whether it is for yourself or a loved one, Beverly Molander and Dave Savage offer a wealth of information in *Heartfelt Memorial Services* on how to endure and honor this transition we call death, and with the utmost respect.
Kent Smith Adams, Certified Grief Recovery Specialist® and Author of *Love Promised: A Future Life Revealed*
UniversalLifeStrings.com

Sometimes the greatest awakening is when death stares us squarely in the face. *Heartfelt Memorial Services* inspires us with unique ideas about how we can bring meaning to end of life experiences for our loved ones and ourselves. It is encouraging to know that we can pick up this guide anytime we need to think clearly about what to do next.
Elise Ballard, Author of *Epiphany: True Stories of Sudden Insight to Inspire, Encourage and Transform* and creator of EpiphanyChannel.com.

Heartfelt Memorial Services is a great book! Thoughtful and insightful, a true gem. I will suggest it for all of my friends and colleagues who are hitting middle age and having to take responsibility for memorial services for loved ones.
Maurice Baker, President, Corporate Volunteer Council of Atlanta cvcofatlanta.org

Beverly and Dave provide great value in their resource guide, *Heartfelt Memorial Services*. It's not so much that they offer a great number of ideas and references, rather it is that they take what is one of the most difficult subjects, the death of a loved one, and provide a simple, gentle road map to guide us. I was particularly pleased to see the materials that address interactions before the death of someone you love, and many suggestions that minimize the awkwardness for those who are most ill at ease. For a passage that is so important for the living, the time is long past due for a book such as this.

Ron Chapman, MSW, Author of *A Killer's Grace*
AKillersGrace.com

I love it and think it is AWESOME – I never dreamed it would be so comprehensive. I can't think of any more to add – you guys did a great job.

Walter Coffey, President, Leading Age Georgia
LeadingAgeGA.org

With grace and gentility Beverly Molander and Dave Savage offer us an important, brilliant book that brings to light and awareness a delicate subject that each one of us is called upon to address at some point in our lives, often unexpectedly—the deeply emotional, profound experience of celebrating and honoring loved ones as they leave their physical presence. The authors take you by the hand, embrace you with love and kindness and understanding, and give you thoughtful, elegant, intelligent, practical guidance at a time when you need it most. I know this book will help so many people in creating a conscious and comforting relationship with the ultimate life transition, making it matter in a sacred experience. This book is a true gift to humanity.

Dianne Collins, Creator of QuantumThink® and Author of award-winning bestseller, *Do You QuantumThink? New Thinking That Will Rock Your World* diannecollins.com

Heartfelt Memorial Services shares considerable knowledge and insight, and I believe this advice will help us to facilitate family participation and maintain our relevance in a changing world.
Elizabeth Fournier, Green Burial Advocate, Owner of Cornerstone Funeral Services CornerstoneFuneral.com

A much needed and loving guide to assist us in times of transition. Beautifully written with heart-centered suggestions and comfort.
Edwene Gaines, Owner of Rock Ridge Retreat Center, Author of *The Four Laws of Spiritual Prosperity* edwenegainesseminars.com

I have nothing but the highest of praise for this book, *Heartfelt Memorial Services*. It came into my life as I was preparing the memorial service for my beloved sister-in-law and it could not have been more inspiring and supportive for me at a difficult time. I praise this collection of thoughtful ideas and inspiration for memorial services of all types. It was a blessing to have so many loving, and meaningful ideas to consider. This book is indispensable to anyone - whether spiritual director, minister, friend or family member to have in their possession. It gave me wonderful support, was relevant and most of all, heartfelt and loving, and supported me in transmitting those qualities through this service. Thank you to Beverly and Dave for providing this invaluable resource.

Dr. Deborah Gordon, Co-founder Centre for Spiritual Living Kelowna, British Columbia cslkelowna.org

Heartfelt Memorial Services is chock full of compassionate, sensible, and helpful advice for dealing with a subject that is impossible for most of us. I am grateful to have this in my library and delighted to recommend it to my friends and clients…an invaluable resource.

M. Marcy Jones, J.D., Author of *Graceful Divorce Solutions*

Heartfelt Memorial Services…is a book that should be in every family's home. Beverly and Dave have taken a very difficult subject and created a compendium of compassionate and practical steps to follow to get you through the process, the entire process, of losing a loved one.

Dr. Dennis Merritt Jones, award winning Author of *The Art of Uncertainty - How to Live in the Mystery of Life and Love It* dennismerrittjones.com

Heartfelt Memorial Services is a richly woven gift for one of life's hardest times, the death of a love one. A must for every minister, pastor, priest and all who facilitate the end of life

services. Complete with samples in all aspects of the loving handling of all the post-death business arrangements, I found myself wanting one to assist me in talking with my mother and siblings as well as my children. Every church and spiritual gathering place will greatly benefit from you sharing your wisdom. This beautiful book will help us openly and lovingly discuss the tender, deeply personal and private end of life time.
Barbara Leger, Founder and Spiritual Director TEMENOS: Center for Self-Realization & TEMENOS: Center for Spiritual Living, Ukraine temenoscsl.org

Heartfelt Memorial Services is comprehensive, providing valuable information, templates and resources to make an otherwise difficult process much easier. The authors take into consideration a grieving family member's reduced ability to function and heightened need for answers and direction.
Lori Anne Rising AuthorshipforExperts.com

Accessible and organized guidance fills the pages of this wise and even entertaining volume. I will recommend this to all who are preparing for peace at life's end. A beautiful memorial service adds grace to the closing line of the story of our lives.
Monica Williams-Murphy MD, Emergency Physician, Medical Director for Advanced Care Planning and End of Life Education Programs Huntsville Area Hospital and Healthcare, Author of *It's OK to Die When You are Prepared* OKtoDie.com

If you are a Celebrant or Funeral Director, grab a cup of coffee and sit back. Beverly Molander and Dave Savage have created an easy to read book chock full of information. *Heartfelt Memorial Services* is a must-have resource if you help families write obituaries, plan personalized services or deliver eulogies. As a bereavement counselor I recommend it highly.
Barbara Rubel, MS, BCETS, CBS, Author of *But I Didn't Say Goodbye* and *Death, Dying and Bereavement*
griefworkcenter.com

For over 75 years, People's Memorial Association has helped people plan for and accomplish simple, dignified, and unique memorial services and funerals. *Heartfelt Memorial Services* is an indispensable and comprehensive compilation of what we've learned and recommend to our families in a single volume, along with things we've still not yet had the chance to include. While there is no "right" or "wrong" way to honor our dead, grieve for them, and mourn, here is a thoughtful, well-considered guide to all of those things. Every person involved in or responsible for planning a memorial of any sort should have access to (and read!) this book, especially professionals in the field.
Rod Stout, Former President and Board Member, People's Memorial Association, Seattle, WA peoplesmemorial.org

Heartfelt Memorial Services is absolutely wonderful! I would consider estate planners and other professionals having this for their clients, as a take away, when discussing end of life issues.

Gift shops should offer this with a tasteful display. Every attorney who does wills should include this in their package. All these people who have free seminars on investing could include this for anyone who makes an appointment for follow up.
Jan Snyder, Business Adviser and person experienced in the loss journey

Years ago, I received a phone call informing me that my previously healthy mate had died on an out of town trip. In the course of a six minute phone call, my world turned upside down. As shattered as I was, I recall confiding in a friend, "I couldn't plan a coffee break at Starbucks right now. How will I ever plan his service?" I wish *Heartfelt Memorial Services* had been in my library at the time. Whether your idea of a grand farewell involves a pub crawl or is more along the lines of high mass, this is a book that helps celebrate life even in the face of death.
Gail Weatherill, RN, The Dementia Nurse, Blog Caregiver Road thedementianurse.com

Heartfelt Memorial Services

Your Guide for Planning Meaningful Funerals, Celebrations of Life,
and Times of Remembrance

© 2015 Memory Keepers Publishing

All rights reserved.

Address inquiries to the publisher:

Memory Keepers Publishing
980 St. Charles Avenue
Atlanta, Georgia 30306

memorykeeperspublishing.com

or connect with the authors directly:

HeartfeltMemorialServices.com
Dave@HeartfeltMemorialServices.com
Beverly@HeartfeltMemorialServices.com

ISBN (print): 978-0-9909808-0-3
ISBN (e-book): 978-0-9909808-1-0

Library of Congress Control Number: 2014960254

First Printing: 2015

Printed in the United States of America

x

Dedication

To my parents, Erma and Shep Savage, and to all of the creative and inspirational extended family of relatives and friends past and present.
-Dave Savage

To my parents, Beverly Stoll Molander Farley and Francis E. Molander,
who taught me about living and dying.
-Beverly Molander

And for each of our children, Laura Savage and Nigel Levine.
May this book make our transition journey easier for you.

Acknowledgments

Woubit Abdela, PhD

Maurice ("Moe") Baker

Margie Baxley

Iris Bolton

Walter Coffey

The Coogle Family

Susan B. Dickey, RN, PhD

Martha Eskew and Chet Tisdale

Broc Fischer

Wendy Haynes

Debbie Kerr

Maureen Killoran

Marq T. Laube Art

Dr. Tom Long

Lorikay Photography

The McCullough Family

Bill Pope

Marie Reeder

Dawn Richerson

Dr. Bernie Siegel

Mari Selby

Terry Sullivan

Bruce Wadd

F. Todd Winninger

Alan Wolfelt, PhD

Sarah York

Table of Contents

Introduction

We all dread making decisions, especially when we don't think we have satisfactory answers or options. This is particularly true when it comes to dealing with the tough issues that surround your loved one's end-of-life journey or unexpected death.

Out of that grief and anxiety comes confusion and lack of direction. *Heartfelt Memorial Services* provides immediate help for making decisions and taking action during such a poignant time. You will also find ideas, resources and advice for making any time of care- giving more significant for your family and your loved one.

You can create heartfelt memorial services or ceremonies any time. Family and friends can gather before their loved one dies; after the death for a funeral or memorial service; or long after the death in a meaningful time of remembrance.

The decline and death of a loved one can be the most stressful time we will go through in our lives. While we will certainly go through a grieving process with each loss, grief can sometimes be deepened by regret. Regret that we didn't take advantage of the time we had left. Regret that we could have handled something differently. Regret that we could have honored our loved one better. Lost opportunities turn into regret. Regret turns into grieving for what could have been.

As Abby Slovin, author of *Letters in Cardboard Boxes*, says, "Grief can put all kinds of regret into focus." While *Heartfelt Memorial Services* cannot relieve you from the grief you feel, we can help ease your pain. We give you things to do so that you have fewer regrets about what you did and how you did it during the caregiving, dying and memorial service process. *Heartfelt Memorial Services* helps you plan during these last life transitions, so that you feel that you have done the best you can under whatever the circumstance.

Heartfelt Memorial Services provides value to families and individuals who:

- need an immediate resource to plan a funeral or memorial service.

- are anticipating and preparing for the death of a loved one.

- want to have "The Conversation" with their elders about end-of-life choices and options.

- are looking for ways to bring together friends and family with a sense of unity and integrity, even when different belief systems may appear to be a stumbling block.

- would like to plan a touching time of remembrance or ceremony after a loved one has died.

- want to create an inspiring celebration-of-life / tribute gathering in honor of a friend while the person is still there to enjoy it.
- wish to ease the burden on the family by planning for your own eventual death.

As co-authors, Beverly Molander and Dave Savage bring experience and expertise from their varied professional backgrounds. Beverly Molander is a minister with Centers for Spiritual Living, an international organization, and is a radio host of a weekly show on Unity Online Radio. Beverly explains, "As a spiritual counselor who has participated in many memorial services and celebration-of-life gatherings, I have felt the intensity, pain and loss of those who are faced with saying goodbye. Those with sad hearts were able to feel a sense of gladness and satisfaction when they felt they 'did the right thing' in honor of their loved one. My goal is to give everyone the opportunity to do the best they can during this trying time, with fewer regrets."

Dave Savage is founder and producer of Memory Keepers Video, a company that helps individuals and families create a legacy through family storytelling and sharing that will be passed on for generations to come. Dave says, "There is heartfelt connection that takes place when people share themselves with each other. In video-taping, the recording of a loved one is one of the most valuable things that can be done. Nothing takes the place of being able to see and feel that loved one, long after the death. If you don't do this, you have lost an opportunity that can never be repeated."

As a congregational leader for 25 years, Dave helped to create and lead many services and ceremonies. Dave adds, "People gain when they are told something or shown something, but when they experience something, the results are deeper and more meaningful. When people have ways to participate, they experience more benefit. In *Heartfelt Memorial Services*, we provide activities that people can do to enrich their lives."

Both Beverly and Dave use the materials in this book when assisting families and acting as funeral or memorial service planners and officiants. They also share their experience and advice as educators to companies and organizations.

Part I of *Heartfelt Memorial Services* is dedicated to the time that many of us dread the most – the death of a loved one. We address your immediate needs when planning a funeral or memorial service. You will gain clarity about what to do and how to do it. There are practical issues to think about and this how-to section can guide you through each phase. You will find out how to notify others about the death, decide on the kind of ceremony you want, select the officiates, write the obituary or eulogy, plan the ceremony, recruit others to help, resolve tricky family matters, prepare for the reception; and be able to navigate these tasks with a better sense of confidence and ease.

Part II is multi-faceted and is about honoring your loved one, either long before or long after the person has died. Relationships don't begin or end with a memorial service. Your loved one can be honored and appreciated whenever you choose. As you anticipate or experience the loss of a loved one, there are connecting and heartfelt things to do and say that will elevate interaction and will help minimize future regrets.

We hear a lot about people who carry around regrets: *I wish we could have talked about these end-of-life issues when Dad was still able to participate; I wish I could hear grandma's voice one more time; I never got to tell Sam how much he meant to us; I wish I knew who we should invite to her bedside and memorial service; Aunt Margaret was the last person who could have explained these old photos to us.*

The beginning of Part II contains many heartwarming activities you can do with your loved one long before death occurs. Why not have a conversation with your loved ones while everyone is still available to participate? The sharing of fond memories and family history will be treasured. *Heartfelt Memorial Services* even shows you how to put together a video recording that will last as a legacy for generations to come.

It's nice to honor a person at a funeral or memorial service, but it can be even better when the person is alive and alert enough to receive all that love and acknowledgment in person. A celebration-of-life gathering is a beautiful tribute for the honoree, and it is also a gift for friends and family: they have a chance to express their love and appreciation directly to the person they admire. *Heartfelt Memorial Services* shows ways to add significance and depth to the gathering that takes it far beyond a simple party. A celebration-of-life gathering is a way to express your love now, while you still can.

For others, a Time of Remembrance is an opportunity to acknowledge the ones who are gone, even years after their deaths. *Heartfelt Memorial Services* shows you ways to personalize your situation, whether you want to honor someone you love or put to rest a bad relationship whose impact lingers.

How to Use Heartfelt Memorial Services

You may be overwhelmed if you try to read this resource from cover to cover. Thumb through and choose the topics that resonate with you, your needs, and your circumstances, at the moment. Since each chapter is designed to stand alone, you may notice that some information is repeated in different forms. Just take the information you want and leave the rest for future consideration, when your heart and mind are in a different place.

Find the Right Words to Say

While researching and writing *Heartfelt Memorial Services*, we found a particularly strong reaction on the subject of insensitive things people say. When talking with someone who is dying, or when wanting to bring comfort to the family and friends of a loved one who died, some people become tongue-tied. Without meaning to, they blurt out something completely inappropriate. There are quotes about that: *Words have wings* (they fly off and cannot be taken back); *Words have feet* (they walk away from the meaning that was intended); *Words that hurt cause pain* (they injure the recipient and damage relationships). Of course these descriptions include those who are grieving, anticipating a loss, have been diagnosed with a life-threatening illness, and more. As a counterpoint to the verbal blunders to avoid, we also include words and actions that people want to hear and experience from you.

Before you read this book, we suggest that you first read our special section on "What Not to Say and What to Say" in Appendix I. This will be beneficial to you, your family, and friends in creating a supportive and nurturing atmosphere.

PART I
Planning and Organizing the Service or Ceremony

The terms "service," "ceremony" and "ritual" are closely related. As a loose definition, a service implies that there is an audience to participate in an ordered set of ceremonies and interactions, perhaps with a religious undertone. A ceremony is similar to a service but provides for more personal preferences in what is done and in the way in which it is done. A ritual is a series of particular actions done in a specific order and often repeated.

CHAPTER 1
Letting People Know

When you are anticipating the eventual death of a loved one, begin by making a list of the people who would want to know if your loved one has passed. From the owner of the local bakery to the cousin who shared summer camp experiences, many people would likely appreciate being notified. Consider all those who may wish to have a chance to pay their respects before the person has died. Below are some of the categories of people you may wish to add to a notification list.

As we know, tragedies strike unexpectedly. It is a real gift for you to start a notification list for your loved ones now. There are many people who care about you, and your family members might never have heard of them. They would not be able to notify them of your passing without your thoughtful preparation in advance.

Family and Friends

Even before their passing, your loved one may have friends to whom they would like to say goodbye. It is valuable to compile a list of your loved one's friends before the end of life.

After the death of a loved one, designate a particular person to make personal contact with those who need to be notified first. If possible, gather address books and Internet passwords in advance, so you can quickly access contact information for those who might need or want to know.

Prior to making personal contact, make notes to ensure that consistent information is provided to each person. Below are typical questions people may have. Consider the answers you wish to provide.

1. When and where did the death occur?
2. What was the cause of death?
3. Had the person been ill for an extended period?
4. What are the details of the wake, funeral or memorial service?
5. Is there visitation before or after the service?
6. Who is invited to attend visitation? (Where appropriate, include dates, addresses, and times.)
7. How is the family doing?
8. Does the family wish to receive visitors?
9. Are flowers, cards or donations welcome? (If yes, provide contact information.)
10. How can someone offer help?

You may wish to refer those who want to help to a volunteer coordinator who will keep track of tasks that need to be done. For a list of potential tasks, see the chapter on volunteering. Keep a head count of those who plan to attend the service so that you can determine the size of the facility and the amount of refreshments that will be needed.

You will have enough stress to contend with as you go through your own grieving process and prepare for the memorial service. If someone does not get notified and is hurt by the oversight, your response to just about everything can be, "I'm sorry. I am doing the best I can."

Imagine:

A friend or relative is rummaging through your desk, drawers and cabinets, attempting to find and make sense of computer passwords and lists and scraps of paper with contact information of people they should notify...

Website to Help Share CareGiving Status and Information

During those last days or months of life, the ones closest to the individual are often overwhelmed with taking care of immediate needs. Communicating with people outside of the inner circle can be cumbersome and time-consuming. In such cases, websites such as CaringBridge (CaringBridge.com) offer a great solution.

On the CaringBridge website, either the person going through a health challenge or a family member can host a page dedicated to communication about the loved one. Instead of having to call numerous folks to keep them abreast of the situation, information is shared through this centralized communication channel.

Guests who are approved by the host can be updated along the way. In turn, those guests can respond and post a supportive message. The CaringBridge website also offers a Support Planner Calendar that helps family and friends coordinate care and organize tasks, such as bringing a meal, offering rides, or taking care of the individual's home or pets. You can also notify guests if the loved one has died.

Groups and Organizations

Was the person part of a group such as a veteran, civic, or fraternal organization? Also consider hobby, sports, religious organizations, health-related interest groups, dance clubs, senior centers, or even the local beauty salon. Where did the person work? Provide notification information that can be used for newsletters or announcement boards managed by these groups and organizations.

Public Notices

Social Media. The Internet is taking the place of newspapers for notifying others of someone's passing. A funeral home handling the body may post a notice on its website. Family and friends will see the link and then provide it to others via social networks such as Facebook and LinkedIn or by e-mail. Online networks also provide a place for posting condolence messages or remembrances for the remaining family. You can post a message on the deceased's Facebook and LinkedIn pages (you will need the user IDs and passwords) as well as the social media sites of some immediate family and friends.

Newspaper Obituary Notices. Timeliness of the notice can be an issue if the newspaper is only delivered weekly. Some newspapers are delivered daily, but since fewer people subscribe, your notice may not be read. Most papers have an online edition, so inquire how you can take full advantage of that.

Local Media. If the person was a prominent member of the community, television or radio news outlets will be interested in reporting on the death.

CHAPTER 2
Writing the Obituary

Obituaries have changed with the advent of the internet. Newspapers charge by the amount of space used, so being brief costs less money. If you post an obituary in a newspaper you might want to refer the reader to a tribute website to find out more.

In longer obituaries there is room to tell more of a story about the person. If your budget allows for a longer newspaper posting, or if you are using a tribute website without space constraints, you may choose to use the following styles. In the examples below, the first is more formal and respectful, while the second adds humor for an unconventional man.

Sample Obituaries

Ken's obituary was placed by the family and provides a professional and personal perspective of the whole man. It was published in *The Atlanta Journal-Constitution* on September 29, 2005.

Ken Coogle, 98, died in his sleep September 23. Born in Kentucky in 1907, he earned a B.S. in biology from the University of Louisville. A job with Southern Bell brought him to Atlanta in the late 1930s. In 1940, he and his wife, Lois Skaggs Coogle, bought their Sandy Springs home, where he lived until his death. During World War II, Ken served in the Navy, developing radar. In the early 1950s, Ken launched Eveready Plastics, a small business making ear molds for hearing aids. Ken retired in 1986, devoting his time to travel with the Friendship Force, tennis, self-hypnosis, and woodworking. Ken was known as a man of integrity, wit, fairness, and well-chosen words, who told good stories, relished good jokes, and made a surprisingly palatable homemade wine. Legendary accomplishments include: Kentucky State Diving Championship, 1933; Tampa Tarpon Tournament winner, 1940; oldest finisher, Peachtree Road Race, 1976; and replicating a 22-foot oak cotton press screw, a 10-year project he completed at age 95 for Historic Westville village. When asked the secret to his hearty longevity, Ken replied, "Curiosity and a daily glass of wine." He donated his body to medical research. Ken is warmly remembered by his wife, Lois; his children, Linda Stephens, Diana Coogle, Sharon Coogle Johnston, Laura Martin Burch, Lee Coogle, and their spouses; eight grandchildren; two (soon three) great-grandchildren; and scores of friends. Remembrance Celebration: October 1, 2 p.m., Peachtree Road United Methodist Church. In lieu of flowers, please send donations to John C.

Campbell Folk School, One Folk School Rd., Brasstown, NC 28902, 1-800-FOL-KSCH; funds support a new wood-turning studio.

This fun and irreverent obituary went viral September 2013. It could almost be used as a eulogy. This obituary was published in *Savannah Morning News* on September 14, 2013.

William Freddie McCullough – The man. The myth. The legend. Men wanted to be him and women wanted to be with him. William Freddie McCullough died on September 11, 2013. Freddie loved deep-fried Southern food smothered in Cane Syrup, fishing at Santee Cooper Lake, Little Debbie Cakes, Two and a Half Men, beautiful women, Reese's Cups, and Jim Beam. Not necessarily in that order. He hated vegetables and hypocrites. Not necessarily in that order. He was a master craftsman who single-handedly built his beautiful house from the ground up. Freddie was also great at growing fruit trees, grilling chicken and ribs, popping wheelies on his Harley at 50 mph, making everyone feel appreciated, and hitting Coke bottles at thirty yards with his 45. When it came to floor covering, Freddie was one of the best in the business. And he loved doing it. Freddie loved to tell stories. And you could be sure 50% of every story was true. You just never knew which 50%. Marshall Matt Dillon, Ben Cartwright, and Charlie Harper were his TV heroes. He was the hero for his six children: Mark, Shain,

Clint, Brandice, Ashley, and Thomas. Freddie adored the ladies, and they adored him.

There isn't enough space here to list all of the women from Freddie's past. There isn't enough space in the Bloomingdale phone book. A few of the more colorful ones were Momma Margie, Crazy Pam, Big Tittie Wanda, Spacy Stacy, and Sweet Melissa (he explained that nickname had nothing to do with her attitude). He attracted more women than a shoe sale at Macy's. He got married when he was 18, but it didn't last. Freddie was no quitter, however, so he gave it a shot two more times. It didn't work out with any of the wives, but he managed to stay friends with them and their parents.

In between his many adventures, Freddie appeared in several films, including The Ordeal of Dr. Mudd, A Time for Miracles, The Conspirator, Double Wide Blues, and Pretty Fishes. When Freddie took off for that pool party in the sky, he left behind his sons Mark McCullough, Shain McCullough and his wife Amy, Clint McCullough and his wife Desiree, and Thomas McCullough and his wife Candice; his daughters Brandice Chambers and her husband Michael, Ashley Cooler and her husband Justin; his brothers Jimmie and Eddie McCullough; his girlfriend Lisa Hopkins; and seven delightful grandkids. Freddie was killed when he rushed into a burning orphanage to save a group of adorable children – or maybe not. We all know how he liked to tell stories.

Short death notices can typically be placed in a local newspaper free of charge. If you want more space for detail, the charge is based on column-inch. We have seen family members go to great lengths to create a beautiful obituary only to discover the cost to place their obituary notice was more than 300 dollars, a price they simply could not pay. Conduct cost research before writing an obituary, considering length and price as you prepare the obituary. One way to save money is to place a short notice in the newspaper that includes a website link to a tribute/memorial site that can be created with the help of:

- the newspaper.
- the funeral home.
- one of many specialized websites.
- a tech-savvy friend or relative.

These tribute sites often include many pictures, stories, and a way for people to leave their love, admiration, and appreciation for the family to read later. Some allow you to include a picture slideshow or video that you may have at the funeral or memorial service.

To get the facts straight, it is helpful to use an old resume or bio for reference and remembrance. If one person writes the obituary, make sure others crosscheck it for accuracy.

Preparing Early

When the writing task falls upon one who is grieving, this can be difficult and time-consuming. We might well take a lesson from major newspapers – they already have obituaries written for major celebrities, dignitaries, community leaders, and politicians. When the person dies, it is only necessary to update and edit the information, not start writing from scratch.

Contrary to the belief of some, writing an obituary in advance is not a death wish. It is similar to writing a will or preparing a document with instructions following your death. This practical and helpful documentation is an act of love that can provide greater ease in a difficult time. The individual who prepares such a document does a great service to those left behind.

What to Include

An obituary can be many things: notice of a death, the story of a life, or a record of the family left behind. Accuracy and completeness are most important. Without proper time and attention given to the obituary, names can be misspelled, dates can be wrong, relatives can be inadvertently left out, and information can be missed. Plan ahead so you will have the time to complete a proper and accurate obituary. Ensure accuracy by proofreading; then let someone else proofread again. Crosscheck information that might be easily overlooked, such as date of death, spelling of the hometown, spelling of sibling names, and the precise number of grandchildren. Don't just assume that your information is correct.

An obituary can often be a warm-up for creating the eulogy that will be offered at the memorial service. Jot down examples of what made that person unique. It might help to list three to five chief characteristics and stick to that. For instance:

- She attributed her longevity to plunging into the Long Island Sound every day, regardless of weather.
- He treated his children to bass fishing lessons.
- He was an authority on all things Judy Garland.
- He started the local barbershop quartet.
- She found homes for more than 150 stray animals.

Consider writing different versions of the obituary. You could have a shorter obituary for a paid classified ad, for example, and a longer version to include in the company newsletter.

Parts of the Obituary

The Basics. We encourage you to select what feels best from the following list:

- Full name of the deceased, including nickname, if any

- Age at death

- City and state of residence at death

- Day and date of death, including the year

- Place of death

- Cause of death – always optional, see below

- Date of birth

- Place of birth and/or hometown

- Childhood schools, friends

- Education (high school, college, university, other)

- Designations, awards, other achievements

- Employment (dates, locations, titles, areas of expertise)

- Places of residence

- Hobbies, sports, interests, activities

- Volunteer, religious, community, or other affiliations and positions held

- Unusual qualities or talents

- Travel

- Survived by – include names and places of residence

- Spouse and former spouses

- Children (in order of date of birth, listed with names of spouses)

- Grandchildren, great-grandchildren, great-great-grandchildren
- Parents
- Siblings, in order of date of birth
- Grandparents
- Nephews, nieces, cousins, in-laws
- Close Friends
- Pets (where appropriate)
- Predeceased by (those who died before)
- Notice of Services – if no public funeral or memorial activities will take place, simply say, "A private ceremony will be held." If a service is planned, give day, date, time, place.
- Name of officiant, pallbearers, honorary pallbearers
- Visitation information: day, date, time, place
- Reception information: day, date, time, place
- Other memorial, vigil, or graveside services: day, date, time, place
- Place of interment
- Name of funeral home in charge of arrangements
- Phone number or website to get more information – include, even if no service is planned.
- Contributions and donations – include contacts, addresses, and websites.

Cause of Death. You may opt to leave this out. We have seen references such as "lost her battle with ___" or "succumbed to ___" which can imply to the reader that the deceased individual was defeated or that she gave up. Death is a unique experience and it will happen to us all, even if we try really hard to stay alive.

Privacy and Security Issues

While caution is a good thing, you must find your own comfort level with the information you are going to release. A few security issues to consider:

Home Address. Do not list the street address of the deceased person. Thieves could conclude that the home may be unoccupied or that the elderly spouse would be defenseless against burglars. They also may be waiting to break in while the funeral or memorial service is taking place. Sometimes burglars monitor the funeral notices to get this information. Consider asking someone to stay at the home during the service.

Date of Birth. Be careful when releasing information like date of birth, as some thieves may be looking to create a new identity with the name of your deceased.

Other Facts about the Deceased Individual. Other criminals could use the personal information to imply a previous relationship with the deceased, eventually causing financial harm. Later on the criminal may try to use this information to take financial advantage of the family.

CHAPTER 3

Deciding on the Style and Scope of the Service

When to Hold the Service

If you are fortunate, your loved one prepared a plan for his or her service. Unfortunately, this is not common. Most of us are left with a lot of questions following their death. What to do? Funeral or memorial service? How many people? Who is in charge?

Sometimes a shorter, simpler service is required. If the death was sudden and loved ones are in shock, they may not be prepared emotionally to plan a larger service. This may call for a smaller funeral near the time of death and a larger, more significant memorial service later, when the focus can be on the joy of the person and not on the sadness of the death. This also allows those who wish to attend time to plan ahead and keep travel budgets under control.

Check to make sure the timing of the service does not coincide with activities, such as major sporting events or festivals that may limit access to the service. Make it as easy as possible for people to attend and for food service, flowers, or affordable lodging and airfares to be obtained. If a public figure has died, you might want to defer the date of the service to accommodate other public figures who want to attend.

Who Plans the Service

Before and immediately after the death, look for any instructions the deceased may have left as to how to handle the ceremony or the body. Is there anything on the computer? In the safe deposit box? In the shoebox next to the scrapbook in the closet?

When no instructions are left, loved ones are often faced with trying to decide what to do. Usually family members or the ones closest to the deceased plan the memorial service. If you are using a funeral home, staff members may be useful in helping you make decisions.

There is also a growing number of trained officiants, also called celebrants, who work independently or through funeral homes. They can help families plan a meaningful service. To find one near you, search the web for funeral officiants or celebrants available in your part of the world.

There can be confusion as to who takes on the primary responsibility for funeral arrangements and planning a memorial service. This is especially the case if relatives have been living far away from the one who has died. It becomes much easier if the family designates a primary decision-maker and contact person.

Put heads together to decide on who this will be. When appropriate, involve relatives close to the deceased and friends or relatives who were close in proximity to the loved one in the planning process.

Open Casket or Closed Casket?
Rental Casket?

Do you have a cultural or religious belief or concern that would cause you to be in favor of or against an open casket? This topic is so emotion-packed it has been known to separate families during this difficult time. It is important to engage in conversation to facilitate better understanding and reach a consensus as early as possible.

Through the ages, many traditions encourage prominently displaying the body in the home or at the mortuary for a period of time before the burial, so visitors can get one last glimpse of their loved one. For some the significance can have a deeper meaning. Some find solace in being able to sit with the body in order to express words or thoughts of regret or love that may have been difficult to say while the person was alive. In more recent times, display of the body has become less popular.

If there are differences of opinion, explore further to find out why key family members feel as they do. The age of the person and condition of the body could have some bearing on the decision. If some family members feel that an open casket is crucial, perhaps holding a wake or viewing at a funeral home could be the best solution.

The open casket could then be closed for the service. You could also put the open casket in another room or behind a screen for those who want to see it. Put a display board with pictures of the person in front of the screen for the others.

An option that is gaining popularity is renting an attractive casket for a funeral service that is held at a congregation or location other than a graveside internment. The body is placed inside of a purchased fiber board or heavy duty cardboard casket that is placed inside the nicer rented casket. The funeral home conceals the inner box with fabric. The inner casket can then be taken for cremation or burial internment.

Research online to find a large selection of printed-design cardboard and other decorative caskets that a mortuary can order. Learn about the required specifications of the liner caskets before ordering or making one yourself. In the United States, the law requires that a mortuary use a provided casket. Of course there will be charges for any additional mortuary services you choose.

Finding Compromise when Opinions Differ

When religious and nonreligious preferences differ, find some middle ground that allows everyone to contribute. There may be differing beliefs around religion and spirituality, between the generations, and even among living family members within the same generation. Consider compromise.

The service is meant to be as inclusive as possible, meeting the emotional needs of those who attend. There are several ways to include a reading or hymn that would satisfy a sense of belonging to a family member with a unique point of view. If you include something from another religious or cultural tradition, explain its significance. For example, "We're including Aunt Emily's favorite hymn because it meant so much to her." Those attending the service do not have to share the aunt's beliefs in order to honor her in this way.

To honor those who are present, the reader could say something such as "For Tim's parents and all of their friends from Greenside Church who are here today..." or "The following poem was one that Tim carried in his wallet..." Offering such brief words of explanation can put mourners at ease and contribute to a service where participants both maintain the integrity of their own beliefs while honoring the beliefs of others. It also encourages people of other faith traditions and nonbelievers to more fully participate in singing religious songs, if they are doing it to be supportive of a grieving family member.

As an example, friends of Dave's had a Jewish identity but were not religious. When their father died, their more conservative mother had certain ideas about how the service and the burial should proceed; however, she was not capable of making the plans herself. The children met with a rabbi and researched online to learn about mourning traditions. They discussed with their mother which traditions were most important to her. They added integrity to the service by announcing that certain parts of the service were being done to honor their mother.

Australian celebrant and author Wendy Haynes suggests finding a clergy or officiant who will remain impartial and mediate between conflicting family members. This can be a valuable consideration when choosing the key facilitator, as many unresolved family issues can be amplified at times of death. Such issues can cause further pain and heartache in a time of heightened stress. The clergy or officiant can facilitate through the challenges and open the way for healing. See the chapter on dealing with family tensions for further suggestions and information.

Deciding on a Budget

While it is wonderful when the service can be paid for by the estate of the departed, sometimes the money is not readily available for use. If there was no will, the money can be tied up in probate for months to come. In such cases, expenses must be covered by living relatives, and the amount of money available may impact how long the obituary will be, where a memorial service is held, who gets paid when, and if programs will be printed.

Where there is no money designated for a funeral by the deceased, services can be paid for by the estate, the executor of the will, or by relatives and friends. If you choose to pay for items before the estate is settled, keep receipts of every expenditure so the estate can justify paying you back. In some countries, there are funds available if the person who died is destitute. In addition, there are financial products that will pay the funeral home in advance of monies that will be released by the state. Be aware that these credit opportunities come with additional expenses and fees. Educate yourself and ask questions before signing on the dotted line.

Money issues that cause friction in families need to be addressed early and forthrightly. Honoring a long-ago plan by the deceased (for instance, "I want to be buried in my homeland.") may not be appropriate now, especially if financial situations have changed for the family members. A potentially volatile issue could be that lavish sums spent on memorial and funeral expenses will not be available for pressing expenses or the debt of the family who will inherit what is left. Deciding family priorities is important for all concerned. Consider the wellbeing of the family and the emotional issues at hand. It may be wise to hire a family therapist or delegate the decision-making process to a third party.

A memorial service budget can include:

- Facility rental
- Staffing for set-up, clean-up, parking, or security (Note: a

service for a celebrity or public figure might require hiring several police for traffic and crowd control.)

- Furniture rental
- Tablecloths
- Clergy or officiant
- Organist
- Soloists or musicians
- Videographer
- Photographer
- Live video streaming
- Program design and printing
- Flowers, rose petals, greenery
- Rental of ceremonial casket
- Products and services needed for a reception

Factors to consider when developing a funeral budget:

- Amount of money available for burial or cremation and memorial service
- Friends or family members who will either gift money or provide deep discounts for the products and services mentioned above

Complications can arise when immediate and extended family members come to provide care or support prior to the death or for the memorial service. They will often stay for several days. Is the expense of this taken out of the estate of the deceased? Will lodging, rental cars, restaurant meals, groceries, and travel expenses be shared by all family members regardless of their financial situation? These questions deserve consideration well in advance.

Selecting a Location

Consider the budget and the number of people who might attend when selecting a location for a memorial service. There are several options. In the list below, we explore the pros and cons of each choice.

Funeral Home. Using a funeral home has its advantages. The employees know how to handle many challenging situations, relieving the family of the burden of the details. Chairs are typically available as is the necessary setup for a casket or cremation urn, a podium, and a speaker system. Parking is also available. Catering might also be provided.

On the downside, funeral homes can appear to be generic, sterile, and cold. Funeral homes usually offer an array of packages and services, like a wedding planner. Time, effort, and money are involved. Just as hiring a wedding planner is often a good investment, hiring a funeral home or independent funeral coordinator to help plan the event will require an investment, but it may be worth it to reduce the emotional cost.

Church or Chapel. You or the loved one might already have a congregation affiliation or a connection from the past. Each faith or denomination may have restrictions that have to be considered. For instance:

- Are there dietary restrictions as to what can be served? As an example, a Jewish Synagogue may require that only kosher food be served.
- Does the service have to be religious in nature?
- Can an independent officiant be used?
- Are there date or time restrictions for using the facility or staff?
- Is liability insurance needed?

Ask for a list of what a particular church or center of worship provides and ask about the budget for each item. There may be a congregational committee that helps manage memorial services. Members of the congregation may take over responsibilities such as directing parking or handling the reception. If church members are expected to show up for the service, get an idea of the number of people expected as their attendance could greatly affect the size and cost of a reception.

Hotel or Restaurant. Hotels and restaurants often have rooms available to rent that can accommodate virtually any size group. Attendees from out of town require sometimes easy access to the airport or to mass transit. These locations can be perceived as cold or impersonal or too informal and disrespectful for the service or ceremony, but they can be just fine for a gathering afterward. Expenses can be high, and catering through the facility may be required. If enough rooms are rented for lodging, some hotels provide a meeting room or family gathering room so people can meet in one spot.

Additional Location Options

Imagine...

Important parts of your loved one's life. Where are the favorite places of nostalgic family gatherings or personal achievements?

The following locations may are places that may be of some significance to the deceased:

vacation home   municipal building atrium

friend's home   lake, brook, beach

museum   rented houseboat

art gallery	community center
summer camp	campground, hiking trail
nature center	ethnic or cultural center
mountain top	theater stage or lobby
amusement park	religious retreat center
recreational park	botanical garden
dinner cruise ship	social hall, dance club
country club	fraternal group facilities

Questions to Ask About Any Location

Is space available?	What is the ambiance of the facility?
Will they allow your own officiant?	Will it accommodate the crowd size?
Is the clergy or officiant available?	Is space available for the reception?
Are there nonmember use policies?	Are there enough bathrooms?
Is guest lodging nearby?	Are there rules for catering?
Are there places to sit or mingle?	Are there rules for decorations?
Is the location easy to find?	Is there space near the site?
Are enough hours available for setup, the event, and cleanup?	Can people use canes, wheelchairs, and walkers?
Is another event booked after yours?	What is the lighting and sun angle?

What are the combined costs?

Is parking available?

Is electricity available for a sound system or videography?

Is there easy access to the space?

Will the sun be in people's faces?

Do you need signage for those coming from other locations?

Consideration for Outdoor Services

Choosing a significant outdoor location can offer another way to honor the deceased individual. Consider an outdoor destination, such as a park, a favorite hillside, or a location with a view of the city that is symbolic of the deceased's love of nature or free spirit. Perhaps around the apple tree she planted when she was first wed? Or by the flower garden where his prize irises bloom?

Here are some ideas to honor someone with a green thumb and/or love of the wilderness:

- Plant a tree or cluster of shrubs.
- Create a path in the woods.
- Ask the nature center what they need most.
- Supply a garden sculpture and plaque.
- Donate a climbing rock for kids.
- Fund a Scout project, perhaps at a nature center or community garden.
- Build or donate a bench or a walking bridge structure.

If you are unable to hold the service at that special place, consider sharing pictures, souvenirs, and memorabilia of the location on a special table at the memorial service. Alternatively, you may wish to include a meditation time with the sounds of the place playing in the background. For example, the sound of the surf and seagulls may instantly remind children of a father's love of the sea.

CHAPTER 4

Planning Key Parts of the Service

The following consists of some standard parts of a memorial service for your consideration. As with other chapters, choose what seems right for you and also appropriate for the venue, audience, and type of remembrance or life-celebration event you are planning.

Sample Order of a Service

1. Background music as people gather and mingle

2. Seating of guests

3. Opening music that signals the beginning of the service

4. For Memorial Service: processional of family members and close friends

5. For Funeral Service: processional of family or military honor guard with the casket or urn

6. Welcome by the officiant, clergy, or service leader

7. Recognition of family members and close significant others by name and relationship (Take care not to omit someone, even if they are not in attendance; and make sure names are pronounced correctly. For instance, a caregiver

of many years may need to be acknowledged. Decide in advance who else in the audience you should also recognize by name, position, or connection to the deceased individual.)

8. Reading or music for transition into the rest of the service

9. Readings by friends or family members

10. Music or song

11. Guided meditation, moments of reflection, or prayer

12. Responsive reading

13. Eulogy

14. Silent meditation or reflection (Announce the length in advance and conclude the silence with a soft transitional sound such as a bell or the fade-in of a recorded or live song.)

15. Music or special song

16. Remembrances (including the reading of remembrances from those who could not attend)

17. If donations are requested for a special charity, have a spokesperson speak about why it is important to the deceased or the family and how the money will be used. The organization will raise more money if it is going toward a specific achievable goal rather than simply the general fund.

18. Parting words, blessing, or benediction

19. Invitation to reception, last gesture of farewell, and instruction on what follows the service (The officiant might remind the audience that the family will need support for a long time. They can mention that a hug, listening ear, visit, phone call, or some offer of support in the future will provide comfort in the weeks and months to come. Writing a note to express appreciation and remembrance of the deceased will also be a comfort to family members.)
20. Recessional (family exits first at the signal from the officiant)
21. Recessional music plays and continues for socializing time
22. The receiving line

The Receiving Line

A few words from the officiant about the receiving line of family members are also in order before the recessional. Let the guests know if there will be a formal line of family for the guests and family to exchange sentiments. Plan where the receiving line should start so the people can mingle most effectively.

Many of you have seen wedding or funeral receiving lines that blocked doorways and restricted alternate ways to move from and around the room. Plan who should be in the receiving line. A dear friend is likely to have a closer relationship than some relatives.

The issue becomes more complicated with multiple mates, spouses, and children from multiple relationships.

Feelings can be hurt by not being included in the recessional or a receiving line. An alternative is to have family members spread out in the reception room. In both cases, it would be a good idea to have nametags and family connection on the tag. When there are many people in the room, family nametags help guests prioritize who they will greet, especially if their time at the service is limited.

We saw one family who got black elastic armbands for family members to help guests find and identify them. Nametags and identification systems can also prevent embarrassment at having to ask who someone is. For example, you may see a relative you knew as a child who is now an adult. Your interaction would be more meaningful if you could see that she was the child of the deceased individual's first family.

Imagine...

Many people are escorting the casket as it is wheeled or carried from the hearse to the graveside. The hearse is parked far enough away from the grave for the mourners to slowly walk and sing a carefully selected song. Many people are touching the casket as it moves along or are holding hands with those who are. A song leader is helping everyone sing together as they move toward the graveside...

The Importance of Processionals and Recessionals

Although it's easy to skip this part of a service or ceremony, a processional is a meaningful way to signal transition into a special or sacred emotional space. It has the same effect as a wedding processional, preparing the participants and the audience for something important that is beginning to take place. Including appropriate music adds even more emotional impact.

Processionals and recessionals are time-honored traditions that add reverence and mark the significance of what is happening and who is being remembered. In some cultures and communities, motorists pull to the side of the road and observers stop and stand in silence when a funeral procession of vehicles passes.

In their 2013 book, *The Good Funeral: Death, Grief and the Community of Care*, two noted funeral experts, theologian Dr. Thomas Long and funeral director Thomas Lynch, strongly advised families to add a processional and recessional to both formal services and simple ceremonies. They recommend that whenever the body is present, it should be escorted by family, friends or community members through each part of its journey, as a symbol of respect and one of many steps to healing.

Getting the body where it needs to go and the living where they need to be is a key theme of Tom Lynch's message. Part of the honoring of your loved one is often the escorting of the body to either the funeral home or the crematorium. Just as you would not send the body of your loved one to the cemetery to be buried by the mortuary and cemetery staff with no family in attendance and nothing being said, why would you send the body of your loved one to the crematory unescorted?

Both the ground burial and the cremation are honorable ways of disposition and should be handled with the same type of honor and ceremony, to move the mourners to a new emotional place. Moving the body to those places in a sacred, dignified and humane manner is a vital part of the funeral.

There are many ways to make the experience more meaningful for everyone. The use of processionals offers one way to involve friends and family who were close to the person who died. This is considered a position of honor and responsibility. Pallbearers can be selected to carry the casket or cremation urn and to escort the body or the cremation remains at the memorial service or the internment.

If there are more people participating in this ceremony than space allows, consider having the pallbearers walk with a hand connecting to the shoulder of the person in front of them. Or you might use long ceremonial ribbon attached to each side so that many hands can be used. A succession of pallbearer groups can also be arranged. Consider extending the time allotted to carrying the casket or moving the body of the deceased from one place to another. The emotional impact on the participants will be enhanced with longer durations for processionals and recessionals.

The journey docs not need to be made in silence. Consider having singing or musical accompaniment during the processional. In the time-honored tradition of the New Orleans jazz funeral, the body is escorted by a sad-sounding jazz ensemble. After the body is delivered to the cemetery and buried, the musicians play lively music, helping the participants get into the swing of life once again.

There are several presentations by the authors of this book available on YouTube that elaborate on these themes. Search NFDA with Thomas Lynch and Dr. Thomas Long. *The Good Funeral* is the name of their book. We encourage you to watch at least one of the videos. Find links to videos on our website.

Service Program

Printed programs help your guests feel a part of the service. Beverly has attended funerals of dignitaries where large, expensive programs were available to a relatively small number of attendees. Did the planners intend to have a small number of programs so they would turn into a collector's item? Did they only intend that the most "important" people or first to arrive would receive programs? Did they misjudge how many would attend?

At this event, most attendees spent considerable time looking for where programs were being distributed. Without a program, those in attendance had no idea what was happening. This was awkward for all who attended the service. One option is to print a top-notch service program for family members and service participants and to also provide a more utilitarian program for all attendees.

The program includes the basics, such as the key parts of the service, the names of those performing each part and, if desired, their relationship to the deceased. Include appropriate instructions if standing is requested for a particular service part. This is visually and verbally signaled by someone who will lead that portion of the service. Also make a notation in the program if applause is encouraged or allowed for a moving musical performance. If a twelve-year-old family member performs, for example, the audience would surely want to clap in appreciation.

Have you ever been to a funeral where the words of poems or songs were not enunciated clearly? The significance of what is being said or sung is lost. If you want the audience to understand and appreciate the meaning of each reading, include the words in the program or an insert. For poems or readings, list the name or title of the piece and the author.

Depending on your budget, programs can range from a simple, folded white program printed on copy paper to a full-color, multi-page book with pictures and historical narrative. Many websites sell downloadable templates or help you create beautiful programs from the photos and written content you provide. Perhaps you can assign the program design to a tech-savvy teen or young adult. The file can be provided by e-mail directly to a local printer. Ensure that you and others proofread and check for accuracy before the program is printed.

As an alternative to the do-it-yourself approach, inquire about programs with your funeral home. Most mortuaries have access to software to create attractive programs and offer program creation as a service to grieving families. Ask to see examples of what they have done. In addition, the administrator or newsletter editor at many congregations is also likely to have template software.

These items could also be used in a detailed program or insert:

- Picture of the deceased, including name, birth date, and date of death
- Pictures of the deceased with loved ones
- Photos of significant aspects of the deceased's life
- Biography of the deceased (similar to the obituary or eulogy)
- Explanation of any unique spiritual or cultural ceremonies or traditions used during the service
- Expression of appreciation for all who have shown concern, sent cards and flowers, brought food to the family, and assisted in other ways

- Instructions for donations to a designated charity in honor of the deceased
- Location and time of open house or reception

CHAPTER 5
Leading or Facilitating the Service

The officiant or celebrant serves as the master of ceremonies for the memorial service. Unlike registrations required for those conducting a wedding, no official state recognition is needed to conduct a memorial service, funeral or other commemorating ceremony. He or she can be a minister, spiritual leader, friend or family member. While some officiants take over major parts of the ceremony, others simply facilitate the transition to each phase of the service.

Finding an Officiant

Individuals who belong to a religious organization, specific congregation, or denomination will find it easier to identify someone to officiate at the memorial service. If ministers or priests are booked, ask for references of retired clergy who may be more available. For those considering a less religious, more spiritual, or humanist service, refer to non-denominational organizations such as Centers for Spiritual Living, Unitarian Universalist, Unity, or a humanist society.

Ask a local funeral home for suggestions or search online for independent funeral celebrants, officiants, or chaplains. For a list of officiants in the US by state and some other countries, search Funeral Officiant Training or Funeral Celebrant Training for organizations that list their alumni. If you are using a funeral home, ask if they have trained officiants on their staff. Two such organization sites in the United States are In-sightBooks.com and FuneralCelebrantCeremonies.com.

Some families choose to designate a personal representative to serve as the officiant. Before selecting a family member, make sure this person speaks well and will hold up during the stressful time of the service. If that person breaks down in tears and cannot continue, have a Plan B in place.

Imagine...

A friend or officiant is leading the ceremony in a park, wearing a colorful tie-dyed shirt and shorts that made up a typical outfit of the person being remembered...

Imagine...

A clergy or officiant dressed in a white or black robe and a decorative stole is leading the formal service...

Attributes of a Successful Officiant

Consider these when choosing an officiant or clergy:

- Is confident and well-organized

- Will accept clear instruction from the family

- Can give clear instructions to participants

- Manages diversity of opinions and challenges well

- Has good time-management skills to keep the service on track

- Uses a clear and animated speaking voice

- Can handle possible glitches (e.g., family member is too bereft to sing the favorite song, sound system breaks down, someone faints)

Responsibilities of the Officiant

The officiant's primary responsibility is to set the tone and the tempo for the service. Preparation is an important part of this responsibility. If the officiant is outside of the family, meet long before the service so he or she can interview family members to glean appropriate information.

Prior to the meeting, family members can consider what is most important to include in their memorial service. The family can provide a biography or résumé and share pictures or stories about the unique and beloved characteristics of the deceased. It helps when the family and the officiant can plan the format of the service together to ensure the service meets the personal desires of the family and is conducted professionally.

Be sure the officiant understands the religious views of both the deceased and the family to ensure that appropriate language is used. For instance, one person may have left instructions not to use the word "God" in any part of the ceremony, while someone else might think it is the responsibility of the officiant to use the Bible and refer to God throughout the service. There are ways to make a compromise on religious content so everyone has a degree of integrity on what is being presented. See the chapter on "Finding Compromise" for more details.

Have you ever attended a service where the officiant didn't actually know the deceased? Names and nicknames can be mispronounced, familial relationships tangled, and anecdotes mangled. Spell out confusing names phonetically after checking with the family for correct pronunciation. Confirm which names to use. Dave's father provides a great example. His given name is Chester, his work buddies call him Chet, and family and friends call him Shep or Sheppie.

Cultural or ethnic terms can add a special touch to the event. Having the officiant speak to grandchildren, using a comment, such as "Your Zayde (grandfather) was very proud of you," can make a big difference. If possible, review what the officiant is planning to say in advance. It is important not to assume that, simply because the officiant has been doing this for a long time, he or she will choose words or phrases that you will appreciate, or pronounce them correctly. If the officiant isn't familiar with the special words, be sure to spell them out phonetically ("Zay-dee"). Don't be afraid to edit or adapt any of the service components. For instance, you may prefer to substitute a term like "Spirit of Life" for "God" or simply leave out spiritual language.

Sometimes there is a feeling of awkwardness if attendees are unsure whether to laugh or clap in appreciation of a musical performance or something that has been said. Should they stand when family members are led to their seats? The officiant can ease the tension by demonstrating the most appropriate thing to do. The family might also consider including such instructions in the program. As we mention in the music section of this book, the service leader can also show the guests when it is appropriate to clap in appreciation. When a child performs or sings, a song it might be supportive to offer acknowledgement with brief applause.

Have the officiant remind the guests about turning off their cell phones before the opening music. He or she can say, "You don't want to be embarrassed about your phone ringing during the service. Please take care of that now." At a memorial service in a funeral home, a staff member usually does this. Back up this suggestion with a notation in the program.

Planning Meeting with the Family

Often, family members are so stunned from the loss that they have difficulty focusing on planning the service. This is where the role played by an officiant is most important. By holding a planning meeting with the family, you can ask the questions and facilitate the meeting so that each person has a chance to think things through and make decisions. Effective brainstorming requires that everyone feels free to share their thoughts and ideas without criticism or intimidation. This includes children, who sometimes have surprisingly good ideas.

Suggestions for a productive planning meeting:

- Assign a good note-taker who will include the name of the person giving the advice or idea or volunteers to perform a task. For instance, if Joe volunteers to find cello music for the processional, he will feel more accountable when this is recorded by the note-taker. Taking notes also ensures tasks are less likely to fall through the cracks. Include the details of the transitions so that participants can review the schedule of events.

- Each person gets to share without being interrupted or encountering negative reactions.

- The order that people share can be related to how easily

they are intimidated or influenced by others. The shy or
easily-dominated can share first.

- Look for ways to involve additional people in the service.
  There will be many close friends and relatives who may not
  want to have the spotlight on them. Remember that more
  than one person could perform a ceremonial task or be
  honored by being included in the task.

Create a detailed, step-by-step agenda for key participants:

- Print an agenda for everyone involved in the activities (this
  is not the program). The more detail the better.

- Include the details of the transitions so that participants can
  review the schedule of events.

- Make sure that there is a person assigned to each task listed
  on the agenda.

- Since there will always be last minute changes, use a pad of
  sticky notes to cover names and to add reminders for
  particular people.

- For some participants, you may want to highlight,
  underline, or circle their part of the service.

Here are some detailed examples:

1) Jan slowly walks up to podium, holding her book of poetry. Sue and Laurie follow her to the podium and stand slightly behind and to the left of Jan and hold hands. Jan reads the poem, and when the three leave the podium they walk over to Grandma, hand the book to her, give her a kiss, and return to their seats.

2) John walks to the podium and introduces the musician and the song that will be sung. He invites everyone to stand and sing along. After the song, John sits in the chair stage left on the podium. Jack moves to the podium.

3) On her way to the podium, Ruth invites her niece and nephew, Cherie and Chase, to come up to the front of the room. Ruth introduces the children, who hold up pictures they colored for Grandma. With Ruth's encouragement, they explain what they drew and why. Ruth invites the next service participants to the podium and escorts the children back to their seats.

Time Delays – For Whom Do We Wait?

For whom do you delay the start of the service and for how long? There are tales of close friends, relatives, or service providers who get lost on the highway, have car breakdowns, are running late (as usual), or face other calamities on their way to an important memorial service.

Timing becomes particularly important when service providers, or officiants, must leave to attend another engagement. Many officiants charge for the additional delay. Typically, their fee includes a 15-minute buffer, but the family will be responsible for additional fees after this brief grace period. Someone must make the executive decision of when to proceed with the service and just make the best of it.

Imagine...

The service leader is standing at the podium in front of a full congregation. There are four empty seats on the front row, and she is glancing at her watch with a concerned look on her face...

CHAPTER 6
Eulogies and Testimonials

Eulogies are therapeutic for the person sharing as well as for guests. They help ground the ceremony and bring life to the memory of the person who has died. This is usually the most important part of the service, where someone very close has the honor of summing up the deceased's life in full. A family member or dear friend may be the appropriate person to speak.

If the service is religious, you may choose a priest or other clergy. Officiants are sometimes called upon to be the presenter of the eulogy. Deciding who delivers the eulogy can be tricky. Those closest to the deceased may well be the most distraught. Choose someone who is accustomed to speaking in public, can work through emotions, and can follow through with this important task.

The eulogist prepares his or her talk in advance. An obituary can serve as an inspiration and provide background references for a funeral eulogy. This source material can also help in keeping timelines and names straight.

While an obituary is more objective, the eulogy offers subjective thoughts and insights into the deceased's life. It can paint a picture of the essence of the person, including the attitude, voice, manner, philosophy, approach to life, interests, passions, and heroic acts or deeds of the individual. In short, a eulogy can capture those characteristics that lead participants to recall and appreciate the uniqueness of that special person. Don't be afraid to use humor, if that is part of who the person was. It helps break the tension of the event.

Writing and Delivering the Eulogy

Here are some tips for writing the eulogy:

- Consider the length of time you have for the service and the eulogy portion of the service, and practice before you stand to deliver.

- Practice (Yes, we are repeating this!) speaking what you have written. Some words that look good on paper could prove as stumbling blocks when said aloud. Decide when to pause and when to look at the audience.

- Create a structure. Will you build from birth to death (chronologically) or from the present back to the beginning (reverse chronologically), or concentrate on the more recent life-highlights of the deceased?

- Write for the ear, not for the eye. Since you will be speaking, make sure that you speak slowly and clearly enough to be easily understood.

- Do not staple pages together. Number pages so you can keep them in order. It is amazing how often pages can get jumbled or dropped at the most critical times.

Tips for the Eulogist

If you are not experienced at public speaking, read straight from your notes, particularly if you think your emotions might get carried away. Have tissues and water nearby, just in case. You might decide to have someone on the sidelines ready to read your presentation if you are unable to complete this difficult task. In formatting, have words in 18-point font size for the printed text so you can see the words more clearly. A rule of thumb is that one minute of nicely-paced talking equals about 140 to 180 words. When printed or written seven to nine words across and nineteen to twenty lines down, your text will be easier to read, especially if you double-space the lines.

Use straight posture, varying eye contact. Speak into the microphone and be clear and succinct. Practice in advance to ensure you don't get so close to the microphone that you "pop your P's." Make sure that the person in charge of sound is ready to adjust the volume if needed. If you are not an experienced speaker, consider having someone sit in the front row to give you subtle signals to slow down, speed up, or wrap up.

The word eulogy means "praise or blessing." Your willingness to help create a personalized, meaningful eulogy is, in fact, a very real blessing. Author, lecturer, and therapist Dr. Alan Wolfelt offers additional tips for those delivering the eulogy:

Be brave. The thought of writing a speech and presenting it in public makes many people anxious. Set aside your fears for now. You can do this. Focus on the person who died and the gift you will be giving to all who knew and loved him or her.

Think. Before you start writing, go for a long walk or drive and think about the life of the person who died. This will help you collect your thoughts and focus on writing the eulogy.

Brainstorm. Spend half an hour (longer if you want) writing down all the thoughts, ideas, and memories that come to you.

Ask others to share memories. A good way to include others in the ceremony is to ask them to share thoughts and memories, which you can then incorporate into the eulogy. Be sure you don't tell a story that someone else will be sharing.

Look at photos. Flipping through photo albums may remind you of important qualities and memories of the person who died.

Write a draft. Once you've brainstormed and collected memories, it's time to write the first draft. Go somewhere quiet and write it all in one sitting, start to finish. Don't worry about getting it perfect; for now just get it down on paper.

Let it sit. If time allows, let your eulogy draft sit for a few hours or a day before revising.

Get a second opinion. Have someone else – preferably someone who was close to the person who died read over your draft at this point. This person can make revision suggestions and help you avoid inadvertently saying something that might offend others.

Polish. Read your first draft aloud. Look for awkward phrases or stiff wording. Improve the transitions from paragraph to paragraph or thought to thought. Find adjectives and verbs that really capture the essence of the person who died

Present your eulogy with love. Now you need to present your eulogy. You may feel nervous, but if you can keep your focus on the person who died instead of your own fears, you'll loosen up. If you break down as you're talking, that's OK. Everyone will understand. Just stop for a few seconds, collect yourself, and continue.

Speak up. It's very important that you speak clearly and loudly enough so that everyone can hear you.

Learn more about Dr. Wolfelt's books, presentations, and services at CenterForLoss.com. (A special selection of descriptive words and phrases to inspire your writing and speaking is found in Appendix II.)

Here is an example of an informal, heartfelt eulogy:

What I Loved about My Mom

"How many of us have taken a simple comment our parent made when we were young and built a lifelong dread from it? Here is how one writer shared that experience:

And here is how my dread came to fruition on this day. A long time ago, when I was a little girl, around eight-years-old, Mom and I were watching some movie... I don't remember the name of it today. In the movie there was a funeral scene and someone on the screen was delivering a nice, heartfelt eulogy.

It was here that my Mom said casually, 'One day, honey, you can do that for me.' Meaning, eulogize her in that wonderful way. Did my mom mean that she was going to die someday? My questioning turned to dread, and from that day forward I ceaselessly worried about my mom dying and what I would say at her funeral. What could I possibly say about someone I loved so much with a roomful of people looking at me, waiting for me to talk?

"Well, the day I dreaded has arrived. Now, what do I say?

"I started brainstorming by making a list of all the things I loved about my mother. In a short amount of time, I had typed four pages, single-spaced. I stopped and looked down at what I was doing and thought, 'This is my eulogy.' This simple list of all-things-Mom was the eulogy I had worried about since I was eight years old. It was so easy. Now, instead of listing all the 130 thoughts I listed, I would share one memory to represent each decade of Mom's sweet time on this earth. The result included tears of happy and sad as well as shared memories from family and friends, just as I hoped for."

Remembrances/Testimonials

Remembrances are most effective when they convey personal stories and observations rather than simply give generic praise. They can become repetitious at a memorial service, so choose people with different kinds of stories to tell. If you want to include remembrances of those who could not attend, ask them to send you their messages in advance of the ceremony. These could then be read and included during this part of the service.

Imagine...

A large sanctuary filled with guests. At the podium are three grandchildren. The oldest introduces the group and each child shares a special memory of Grandma. "She taught me how to sew," says one child. "She taught me how to catch a fish," shares another. And the littlest one shouts, "COOKIES!" There is a round of laughter as many guests remember those delicious cookies, too...

While attending a recent celebration-of-life service for a dignitary, we noticed that, although the minister gave clear instructions about taking only two minutes for a testimonial, speakers took their time. The first person to share stayed relatively close to the two-minute limit, while those toward the end of the time designated for testimonials shared significantly longer. The final person spoke for nearly twenty minutes.

There is a fine line between saying what needs to be said and taking too long to say it. It is especially important to stay within designated timeframes to accommodate other schedules like obligations of the hired professionals, airline schedules, or food to be served. To avoid this problem, give speakers a heads-up about how long they will be able to speak. The officiant can also announce clearly that someone will stand next to the speakers when it is time to conclude their sharing.

> ### Imagine...
>
> *The same TV or video screen that was used to show photo and video highlights of your loved one before the service is now being used for live Skype video remembrances from relatives who have gathered in another part of the world...*

Sharing from the Audience

The officiant can describe the sharing process beforehand. Set a time limit, and then let the audience know how long this part of the service will last. Arrange in advance to have presenters with remembrances who have agreed speak first so they can set the tone and tempo. To save time, ask speakers to line up to be ready to quickly come to the podium.

One option is to have volunteers hand microphones to those sharing from their seats. The volunteer must hold and maintain control of the microphone. This helps control the amount of time the speaker will take.

If wireless microphones will be used, make sure new batteries are installed to assure proper performance. Low battery life can cause choppy sound and unwanted noise that distracts attention during the service.

Before the service, ask a volunteer to assist a hesitant person in crafting a message if they are not skilled at expressing themselves. You may also want to have someone available to act as a reader for someone who is too nervous, shy, or distraught to speak clearly and concisely. As we said before, you can arrange to have others stand with the speaker in support of them and as they are sharing.

We were at a service where the loving teenage granddaughter had wonderful things to say about her grandfather. She burst into tears as she spoke of a special time. Her mother stood and put her arm around her daughter and gave her all the time she needed to compose herself before she was able to continue. What she wanted to say was important to her, and she had an opportunity to do it. This was one of the most poignant parts of the service.

If appropriate, during the service, announce that there will be a microphone available at the reception for those who want to share at that time. A videographer can record the sharing at the service and during the reception, as well, if desired. Use wireless microphones at the reception to help avoid the big room echo that can happen in social halls.

Ways to Involve the Audience

Here is an engaging exercise that involves and engages most all attendees:

Who Among You?

This activity involves the audience and provides insight and impact. It also takes less time than remembrances. It is most impactful with a large group of guests that come from a diverse range of guest connections to the person who died. The leader asks people to stand or raise their hands when asked "Who among you?" for the following shared connections or memories. Obviously, you will come up with ones that relate to your loved one. Here are several options. Who among you. . .

Imagine...

A large sanctuary filled with guests. Twenty people grin and stand when asked, "Who among you ever played golf with Joe?"

- is related to him?

- toured his garden?

- got an annual birthday call from him?

- volunteered with him on a committee?

- ate some of his delicious pie?

- shared one of his famous hugs?

- sang with him?

- worked with him on a social action project?

- was his student?

- served with him the board of many charities?

- was his employee?

- received advice from him?

- was a supplier to one of his companies?

- went on one of his fishing trips?

- played with him on a team or at the court?

This exercise greatly enhances the way the guests mingle and share at the reception afterward. An alternative to this exercise is to request a short story or interaction from a guest who knew the person at various life stages, such as in early childhood, during high school or college, when he lived in Boston, or after retirement. You can also have people come to the memorabilia table, or bring objects from the memorabilia table to the podium, to explain the significance of the objects and pictures on display. Each item represents a significant story that adds depth to sharing-of-the-journey of the loved one's life.

This simple act can help unite everyone in the audience: "Hold hands with the person to the left of you and to the right of you. Feel the connection we have to (insert name of deceased) moving through each of us, one to the other."

With a song leader, guests are invited to circle the grave and sing some songs that are meaningful for the deceased and the family. The song lyrics are printed on a sheet that may also include other graveside service material, a message from the family, and perhaps even a message from the loved one. Invite one or more people to stand next to and perhaps hold hands or put their hand on the shoulder of the person sharing a common remembrance, sharing a reading, or singing a special song.

Imagine...

A processional of family and friends is coming down the aisle, each holding a memorabilia item. As they come to the memorabilia table in front of the guests, they share the story of their object's significance before placing it on the table...

Another idea is to have attendees carry ceremonial objects in the procession:

- Start out with an empty memory table before the family processional. Successive people in the processional carry and fill the table with objects, and perhaps share with the audience their significance. The first might lay down the cloth for placing the urn, explaining that this was a blanket that Grandma made for little Jess when he was born.

- Light candles, which each person is given, while another person provides opening words.

- Individual flowers, flower petals, candies, or others small items significant to the deceased can be handed out as people arrive, to be later placed in the grave.

- At a graveside service, after the lowering of the casket or placing the cremation remains container in the hole, participants can drop things in the hole as one of the ways of closure. Participants can do this in succession or with a large group as they are moved to do it. The facilitator lets people know that they can do it in silence or share a memory. In Jewish and Islam tradition, the dirt is dropped in by hand or by shovel. Having several hand scoops or shovels on hand helps a large group do this more effectively.

CHAPTER 7

Readings for the Officiant and Presenters

Once you have decided the kind of service you want, it is easier to select suitable readings. Here are some questions to consider:

- Do you want the pieces to be listed or written out in the program?
- Will someone read them aloud?
- Will there be responsive readings, where an individual reads a segment and the guests respond?
- Perhaps an old college friend has a letter from the deceased that sparkles with the personality of that person.

When using a reading, poem, or lyrics to a song, choose the section most appropriate for your situation and leave out the rest. Readings usually last a minute or less. Modify a reading to suit your audience and your time frame. Consider revising the wording to personalize the original work, but be sure to acknowledge the original source and state that you have altered the original. Changing complex words will help keep it simple for the person reading it. Also, keep the length short enough so people won't start shifting in their seats.

Even if the speaker has memorized her reading, he or she can go blank at the last minute, so having something in writing can help save the day. We've all seen baseball games where the celebrity singing the national anthem forgets the words under stress.

If you want to have a favorite poem read at a memorial service, consider whether the audience will understand it. If the words are too lofty or the cadence is off, this can make it difficult for the poem to be appreciated. Perhaps this would be a good poem to use in the program rather than have it read aloud.

Beverly recalls one occasion when the departed was someone who loved Ralph Waldo Emerson's essays. Although the writings were beautiful, they had been written in the late 1800s and the language was not easy to absorb. The person assigned to this task struggled through the entire essay. Audience members felt like they were trapped in a classroom with a monotonous teacher. As such, the significance was lost.

We have included readings that can be used by anyone, including those who describe themselves as spiritual, earth-centered, nonreligious, people-centered, agnostic, or even atheistic. Even in a religious service, one of these readings could be used by the clergy to accommodate some family members and guests. Edit the readings to meet your needs.

Please note that we were unable to find and credit the original authorship for some of the readings we have included. Some have been adapted, edited to suit our preferences and style. If you can show that you deserve credit for any piece included in our book, website, blog, or articles, we will gladly include your full contact information.

Opening and Closing Remarks for Officiants

Choose phrases like: My name is NAME (provide your title or relationship to deceased). It is my privilege to officiate at this important event. We are here to experience together a memorial service, not a funeral. We are here to celebrate a life. While a deep sadness and loss may be present, today we commit to memory the uniqueness and the spirit of our beloved.

Your presence here is both a tribute to the departed and a ministry to the living. We truly honor NAME, who you have known as a beloved relation, a true friend, a beloved colleague, or someone who has touched your life in some special way.

We are celebrating the life of NAME, which perpetuates itself in each of us – as we are all participants in one inter-connecting life. From time-to-time, we come face-to-face with reality, and this is the reality of the departure of a loved one. This time of remembrance is important because this is the only way to move from (unbearable) grief to a serene and fulfilling life.

I know that you deeply miss NAME. But, wouldn't it be strange if you did not? Your sense of loss is a sign of love, not a mark of tragedy. There is an empty place in your heart. Let that place become a safe haven where you go to remember, to rejoice, and to be strengthened.

We meet here today to (celebrate / honor / pay tribute to) the life of NAME and to express our love and admiration for him. We welcome one and all. You belong here because he belongs to you in some unique way. The world is a community, and NAME has been a part of that community. We are all involved in the life and death of each of us.

Human life is built on care, and that is what brings us here together today. We care about NAME and we care about those who are left grieving him (or her). Through the death of a man (or woman) we knew and cared about, each of us is joined to all the others here by our links of kinship, love, or friendship. We have our common bonds, and we are grateful that we can recognize those bonds, even in the midst of our grief.

In this place, we have the opportunity to join in taking leave of someone we have loved – someone for whom we have had the greatest affection and respect, but it is more than that… Though no longer a visible part of your lives, she will always remain a member of your family or your circle, through the influence she has had on us and the special part she has played in our lives.

We know that the value and the meaning of life are found in living one's life and living it well. Our comfort of having a friend, sister, mother, aunt, colleague (choose which relationships are appropriate) may indeed be lost, but the comfort of having had her all of our lives is never lost. Even as we grieve, we can still experience a joy where we can become especially aware of this moment. Fix a living image of NAME in your mind and recall the personal qualities that made her unique. And then smile at that image you have created and keep it close to your heart.

I don't think there is anyone here who does not feel enriched by having known NAME. She will be remembered as a mother, mother-in-law, grandmother, great-grandmother, and friend (choose appropriate relationships). Here are some of the qualities you may remember. (List and describe particular qualities. Note: Plan in advance if you want to involve audience members in this. Make sure they can be heard by the group, and use microphones if you are recording the service.)

We have come together from near and far, from many states, from many lives, drawn together by a need to celebrate life, to celebrate family, and to observe the circle of life (recognize people in the audience, ages, birthdays, anniversaries).

We have traveled to this place to be counted and to say by our presence, "I am me, separate and unique, but I am also part of this family who grieves for this loved one today." And in this quiet time of our busy weekend we draw together to observe the saddest part of life's circle, the loss of one of our own. To remember NAME, and to fulfill the obligation and privilege of family members to support, console, and comfort (name closest family members) and each other at this difficult time. are appropriate for you. The following are some ideas as you prepare your remarks:

Readings for Various Uses

Invocation

We come together from the diversity of our grieving,
to gather in the warmth of this community,
giving stubborn witness to our belief that in times of sadness,
there is room for laughter.
In times of darkness, there always will be light.
May we hold fast to the conviction that what we do with our
lives matters
and that a caring world is possible after all.
~ Maureen Killoran, Unitarian Universalist minister

Litany of Remembrance

This responsive reading can be adapted for individualized
phrases or number of participants.
The celebrant or others could read the (One) refrain
individually.
(One) In the rising and the setting of the sun

(All) We remember NAME

(One) In the blowing wind and the chill of the winter

(All) We remember NAME

(One) In the opening of the buds and the rebirth of spring

(All) We remember NAME

(One) In the clear blue skies and the warmth of summer

(All) We remember NAME

(One) In the rustling of the golden leaves of autumn

(All) We remember NAME

(One) When we have joys and yearn to share

(All) We remember NAME

(One) When we are weary and in need of strength

(All) We remember NAME

(One) So long as we live, he, too, shall live, for he is a part of us.

(All) We remember NAME

(One) In these, and in many other ways, we remember him.

(All) Amen.

~ Traditional Jewish mourning reading, adapted

Feel No Guilt in Laughter;

Feel no guilt in laughter; he'd know how much you care.

Feel no sorrow in a smile that he is not here to share.

You cannot grieve forever; he would not want you to.

He'd hope that you could carry on the way you always do.

So, talk about the good times and the way you showed you cared,

The days you spent together, all the happiness you shared.

For if you keep those moments, you will never be apart

And he will live forever locked safely within your heart.

~ Unknown

Let the Memories Surround You

As long as we can love each other, and remember the feeling of love we had, we can die without ever really going away. All the love you created is still there. All the memories are still there. You live on… in the hearts of everyone you have touched and nurtured while you were here… death ends a life, not a relationship.

~ Mitch Albom, quoting Morrie Schwartz in *Tuesday's with Morrie,* 1997, MitchAlbom.com

Note: Watch an inspirational and moving, 23-minute video from Mitch about Morrie and what he learned from him at MitchAlbom.com/d/film/3729/tuesdays-morrie. Mitch shares many "Morrieisms" you may want to share and learn from.

New Beginnings

New beginnings bring to mind old and recent endings. We owe much to the past and to those who embodied it. Parents and grandparents, children and siblings, teachers and shapers, friends and loved ones – all these, living and dead, add their touch to the person we have become.

To the living, we turn in gratitude and love, extending arms of friendship, offering them renewed love. To the dead, we turn in memory, affirming their lives with the fullness of our own.

~ Unknown

Meditations on Mourning

Strange is our situation here upon earth. Each of us comes for a short visit, not knowing why, yet sometimes seeming to divine a purpose. From the standpoint of daily life, however, there is one thing we do know: that we are here for the sake of each other, above all, for those upon whose smile and well-being our own happiness depends, and also for the countless unknown souls with whose fate we are connected by a bond of sympathy. Many times a day I realize how much my own outer and inner life is built upon the labors of others, both living and dead, and how earnestly I must exert myself in order to give in return as much as I have received and am still receiving.

~ Albert Einstein

Immortality

We are part of a cosmic process, some larger-evolving reality of which we know not the beginning or the essence or the end. We die, but we live on. Our immortality lies in the lives of others. And when we touch their lives creatively and lovingly, we have lived a life worth living.

~ Unknown

The Acorn

A rabbi was passing through a field when he noticed an old man who was planting an acorn.

"Why are you planting that acorn?" he asked. "You surely do not expect to live long enough to see it grown into an oak tree."

The man replied, "My grandparents planted seeds, too, that I might enjoy the shade and the fruit trees. Now I do likewise for my grandchildren and all those who come after me.

And that's how our beloved NAME lived and planted seeds for us.

~ Jewish Talmud, Tanit 23a, paraphrased

She is Gone

You can shed tears that she is gone
Or you can smile because she has lived
You can close your eyes and pray that she will come back
Or you can open your eyes and see all that she has left
Your heart can be empty because you can't see her
Or you can be full of the love that you shared
You can turn your back on tomorrow and live yesterday
Or you can be happy for tomorrow because of yesterday
You can remember her and only that she is gone

Or you can cherish her memory and let it live on

You can cry and close your mind, be empty, or turn your back

Or you can do what she would want: smile, open your eyes,

love, and go on.

~ David Harkins, 1981, Silloth, Cumbria, UK

What Is Success?

To laugh often and love much;

To win the respect of intelligent persons

And the affection of children;

To earn the approbation of honest critics

And to endure the betrayal of false friends;

To appreciate beauty;

To find the best in others;

To give of one's self;

To leave the world a little better,

Whether by a healthy child,

A garden patch

Or a redeemed social condition;

To have played and laughed with enthusiasm

And sung with exultation;

To know that even one life has breathed easier

Because you have lived –

This is to have succeeded.

~ Ralph Waldo Emerson

The Measure of a Man

The measure of a man is not determined

By his show of outward strength

Or the volume of his voice

Or the thunder of his actions

Or of his intellect or academic abilities

It is seen rather in terms of the love that he has

For his family and for everyone

The strength of his commitments

The genuineness of his friendships

The sincerity of his purpose

The quiet courage of his convictions

The fun, laughter, joy and happiness he gives to his family and
to others

His love of life

His patience and his honesty

And his contentment with what he has.

~ Grady Poulard, adapted

Destiny

To him there will be no monument of stone

Nor heraldic cries of achievement past

Just farewell, to see his ashes strewn

But in our sadness we will remember this

His legacy lives on in his children and grandchildren and dear
friends
His endearing smile and good kind ways reflect in them
His destiny is fulfilled and fond memory assured
We will remember him.
~ Unknown

A Mother's Love
Our Mother's love was something that no one can explain
It's made of deep devotion and of sacrifice and pain
It is endless and unselfish and enduring come what may
For nothing can destroy it or take that love away
It is patient and forgiving when all others are forsaking
and it never fails or falters even though the heart is breaking
It believes beyond believing when the world around condemns
and it glows with all the beauty of the rarest, brightest gems
It is far beyond defining, and it defies all explanation
those are the memories we treasure
You have loved us beyond measure.
~ Helen Steiner Rice (1900-1981), American poet

Father
Our father was always a friend,
a wonderful someone on whom we depended.
Sometimes a comforter, quieting fears,

sometimes a banker when we were in arrears,

sometimes a mender of trolleys and bikes,

sometimes a vigorous leader of hikes.

A teacher, a gardener, a plumber of sorts,

a barber, a chauffeur, an expert on sports;

a Jack-of-all-trades, as the old saying goes,

and loved and respected more than he knows.

Just a wonderful dad who always showed

what a wonderful father can be.

~ Unknown

Death Leaves a Heartache

Death leaves a heartache no one can heal,

Love leaves a memory no one can steal.

Life brings tears, smiles and memories.

The tears dry, the smile fades,

but the memories live on forever.

Gone from our sight, but never our memories.

Gone from our touch, but never our hearts

Although no words can really help to ease the loss we bear,

You are very close in every thought and prayer.

~ Unknown

Every Time We Make the Decision to Love Someone

Every time we make the decision to love someone, we open

ourselves to great suffering, because those we most love cause us not only great joy but also great pain. The greatest pain comes from leaving. When the child leaves home, when the husband or wife leaves for a long period of time or for good, when the beloved friend departs to another country or dies… the pain of the leaving can tear us apart.

Still, if we want to avoid the suffering of leaving, we will never experience the joy of loving. And love is stronger than fear, life stronger than death, hope stronger than despair. We have to trust that the risk of loving is always worth taking.
~ Henri Nouwen

I Know for Certain

I know for certain that we never lose the people we love, even to death.
They continue to participate in every act, thought and decision we make.
Their love leaves an indelible imprint in our memories.
We find comfort in knowing that our lives have been enriched by having shared their love.
~ Leo Buscaglia, *Fall of Freddie the Leaf* , LeoBuscaglia.org

A Tear in the Ocean

I dropped a tear in the ocean. The day you find it is the day I will stop missing you.

~ Unknown

Candle Lighting

As the darkness of our loss calls us to community,
Let there be light.
Let the light of this flame remind us of the light of love that NAME shined onto us.
Let there be light.
Let the glow of this flame encourage us to pick up the lantern of (love) that NAME represented,
Let there be light.
Let us shine NAME's love and thoughtfulness, as well as our own onto the lives that we touch.

~ Dave Savage

Stars of Radiance

There are stars whose radiance is visible on earth though they have long been extinct.
There are people whose brilliance continues to light the world even though they are no longer among the living.
These lights are particularly bright when the night is dark.
They light the way for human kind.

~ Hannah (Szenes) Senesh (1921-1944), assisted in rescuing Hungarian Jews, captured and shot 1944

Radiant Stars (Adapted)

There are stars whose radiance is visible on earth though they have long been extinct.

There are people whose brilliance continues to light the world though they are no longer among the living.

Come into the circle of compassion, memory, and love.

Come into the circle of grief and mourning and celebration.

For death has gathered us here to remember NAME, to grieve his/her dying and celebrate the gift of his/her life.

~ Hannah Senesh, adapted by Unknown

Pay Tribute to Our Loved Ones

Memory is what we have to help fill the emptiness left by the passing of those who once brought wholeness to our lives. But memory can only remind us of who we were with those we loved. It can't help us find what we must now become. Those who are gone, still echo within our thoughts and words. Some of what they did is part of what we have become and will strive to be.

We pay tribute to our loved ones when we live most fully. I renew my commitment to honor you, NAME, in the way I follow your best examples of a live well lived.

~ Unknown

Death Has Come to Us Once Again

Death has come to us once again.

We look into our hearts

We speak to our friends

We cry out at night for answers that never satisfy.

Strength exists within us

Support comes from those around us.

From me, from you

But there is only the answer of hope, love, and time

Death is everywhere

But so is life.

~ Unknown

One More Link in the Chain of Our Lives

As we are gathered here with mixed feelings of loss and in celebration of a memorable life, we also think about other loved ones who are not here today. They, too, are a part of us and we feel their presence even now.

A child's gesture recalls that of a grandparent he never knew. An act of kindness and generosity reminds us of the example of a much-loved aunt or uncle. The laugh of one recalls, for us, the joy of another.

A chain of memory and blood binds us, one to another, thru the years and through the generations.

~ Unknown

My (Brother)

He worked hard. He lived simply.

He gave generously to his family and for peace and justice.

No degrees adorned his walls.

No doctorates bore his name.

NAME learned through living, and we learned by watching

him live.

The memories, the influence, the example –

His presence was uniquely NAME.

Father, brother, cousin, and friend.

May his life be a lesson for us all.

A life that taught us by example.

~ Unknown

Dad

Dad gave us himself, his standards and values, his gentleness,

his strength, his humor and love. He shared our lives, our joys

and sorrows, and *we* are the first links to his immortality.

~ Unknown

The Craftsman

(Electrician)

He measured wires and cut them to size;

He stripped and twisted; following with his eyes

The conduit, he begged it to be true;

He joined the plugs and lights until at last there grew

A oneness between the man and electric energy.

He connected us to the energy of the world.

~ Unknown

(Woodworker)

He measured boards and sawed them to the size.

He nailed and pounded; following with his eyes

The hammer stroke, he begged it to be true.

He sanded, polished, until at last there grew

A oneness between the man and wood

He loved the aroma of wood in the air.

His shop was his oasis of tranquility.

~ Unknown

Hold Fast

We want for NAMES and RELATIONSHIPS (Bob and Janice and all the cousins) the courage to continue to hold fast to one another in this time of sorrow. Beyond the ties of family are all of you, the extraordinary family of friends-of-a-lifetime. May we all carry forward the goodness, the love, and the courage of NAME, whose life and death has brought us together.

We enter this world as an unknown to those who await us; and we depart having created our own story of being, a web of relationships, and a treasure of life experiences. We have experienced a bigger and better life because of NAME.

~ Unknown

Closing Words or Benediction

We would like to extend our sincerest gratitude to all family and friends for their loving, gentle support and offerings of solace, company, and assistance. (Choose appropriate mentions) are among those who have helped to carry us through this sorrowful passage. We are deeply grateful to you all.

It is done. We have bid-loving farewell to NAME.

We are glad that we saw her face and felt the glow of her friendship and love. We cherish the memory of her words and deeds as well as her character. Carrying her in our hearts, let us now proceed from this place in comfort and in peace, assured that even in this time of loss and sorrow, life remains precious and good. May we also on this day rekindle in our hearts an appreciation for the gifts of life and of those still among us. Let us honor the life of NAME by living ourselves, more nobly and loving in the days ahead. We return to the routines of our lives. Go in love, and may an abiding peace go with us.

~ Larry Reyka, adapted, deceased chaplain American Humanist Association, Humanist-Society.org

Readings from the Perspective of the Deceased

Farewell My Friends

It was beautiful as long as it lasted, the journey of my life.

I have no regrets whatsoever, except the pain I've left behind.

Strong arms held me up when my own strength let me down.

At every turning of my life I came across good friends, friends who stood by me as I stood by them.

Farewell, farewell, my friends; I smile and bid you goodbye.

Shed no tears for me; all I need are your fond memories and smiles.

If you feel sad, do think of me and how you can share your love of me with those you love.

In that way my love does last.

~ Rabindranath Tagore, adapted

Remember Me

If, when we got together,

Laughter came along,

Remember me.

If, when our minds met,

There were sparks of light,

Remember me.

If, when you felt a need,

And there was warmth and giving,
Remember me.
If any aspect of my life enriched yours,
Nurture it.
Don't mourn my short years,
They were rich and full.
While it was given me, I chose life.
For all that, remember me.
~ Unknown

Afterglow

I'd like the memory of me to be a happy one.
I'd like to leave an afterglow of smiles when life is done.
I'd like to leave an echo whispering softly down the ways,
Of happy times and laughing times and bright and sunny days.
I'd like the tears of those who grieve, to dry before the sun;
Of happy memories that I leave when life is done.
~ Helen Lowrie Marshall

Do Not Grieve

Though I'm gone do not grieve and shed mournful tears
And hug your sorrow to you through the years
But start out bravely with a cheerful smile;
And for my sake do all the things the same
Feed not your loneliness on empty days

But fill each working hour in useful ways

Reach out your hand to others in comfort and cheer

And my memory will comfort you and ease your fears.

Do the things we planned to do

And always remember how much I loved you.

~ Unknown, adapted by Dave Savage, reprinted from UK

funeral website LastingPost.com

High Flight (from a pilot's perspective)

Oh! I have slipped the surly bonds of earth

And danced the skies on laughter-silvered wings;

Sunward I've climbed, and joined the tumbling mirth

Of sun-split clouds – and done a hundred things

You have not dreamed of – wheeled and soared and swung

High in the sunlit silence. Hovering there,

I've chased the shouting wind along, and flung

My eager craft through the footless halls of air.

Up, up the long, delirious burning blue

I've topped the windswept heights with easy grace

Where never lark, or even eagle flew.

And, while with silent, lifting mind I've trod

The high untrespassed sanctity of space,

Put out my hand, and touched the face of God.

~ John Gillespie McGee, Jr., pilot who died in a WWII midair

collision at age 19

Remember Me

To the living, I am gone.

To the sorrowful, I will never return.

To the angry, I was cheated,

But to the happy, I am at peace,

And to the faithful, I have never left.

I cannot be seen, but I can be heard.

So as you stand upon a shore, gazing at a beautiful sea –
remember me.

As you look in awe at a mighty forest and its grand majesty –
remember me.

As you look upon a flower and admire its simplicity –
remember me.

Remember me in your heart, your thoughts, your memories of
the times we loved, the times we cried, the times we fought, the
times we laughed.

For if you always think of me, I will never be gone.

~ Margaret Mead

Do Not Stand at My Grave and Weep

Do not stand at my grave and weep;

I am not there. I do not sleep.

I am a thousand winds that blow.

I am the diamond glints on snow.

I am the sunlight on ripened grain.

I am the gentle autumn rain.
~ Mary Elizabeth Frye (1905-2004), 1932

Death Is Nothing at All

Think of me as if I have only slipped away into the next room
Whatever we were to each other
We are still that
Call me by my own familiar name
Speak to me in the easy way you always used
Put no difference into your tone
Wear no forced air of solemnity or sorrow
Laugh as we always laughed
At the little jokes we always enjoyed together
Let my name be ever the household word that it always was
Let it be spoken without effort
Without the ghost of a shadow in it
Life means all that it ever was
There is absolute unbroken continuity
What is death but a negligible accident?
Remember me well.
~ Henry Scott-Holland (1847-1918), adapted

A Life Well Lived

My life well lived is a precious gift
Of hope and strength and grace,
I hope I've made our world
A brighter, better place

It was filled with moments, sweet and sad
With smiles and sometimes tears,
With friendships formed and good times shared
And laughter through the years.
My life, well lived, is a legacy
Of joy and pride and pleasure,
A living, lasting memory
I wish your grateful hearts will treasure
~ Unknown

Miss Me, But Let Me Go

I have come to the end of my road,

And the sun has set for me,

I want no rites in a gloom filled room

Why cry for a soul set free?

Miss me a little - but not for long.

And not with your head bowed low.

Remember the love that once we shared.

Miss me, but let me go.

For this is a journey we must all take,

And each must go alone.

When you are lonely and sick at heart,

Go to the friends we know,

Laugh at all the things we used to do.

Miss me, but let me go.

~ Edgar Albert Guest, adapted

Quotes

Speak freely of her to her family and friends and share your remembrances with them. To speak not of her tends to deny her existence; to speak freely of her tends to affirm her life.
~ Iris Bolton

We cannot control what happens to us but we can take charge of how we respond. We can choose to survive or we can choose to be devastated. I can no longer change the destiny of my loved one, but I can be sure that my life will be more meaningful as a result of this experience. I can survive. Albert Camus said so beautifully, "In the midst of winter, I finally learned that there was in me an invincible summer."
~ Iris Bolton

As we journey through this life we leave our footprints wherever we go.
~ Unknown

As many are my tears that flow, they cannot wash away the love I have for you. I may not be able to look up and see you, but I can look into my heart because you have left a part of you there.
~ Unknown

Her life philosophy was, "Your life is an occasion. Rise to it."
~ Suzanne Weyn, *Mr. Magorium's Wonder Emporium*
These days are the winter of the soul, but spring comes and
brings new life and beauty, because of the growth of roots in
the dark…
~ Sarah Graves Reeves

Words for a Young Child or Baby
We gather to remember NAME and help each other grieve her
death.
She had grown only a little; but she was an important person in
the hearts of those who loved her.
Such a little child/baby made a huge impression of love for
those who knew her during her short, short life.
Such a big impression when she had such little time among us.
~ Unknown

The Unfinished (for a young person)
We cannot judge a biography by its length
Nor by the number of pages in it,
We must judge it by the richness of its contents,
Sometimes those unfinished are among the most poignant.
We cannot judge a song by its duration
Nor by the number of its notes,
We must judge it by the way it touches and lifts our souls,

Sometimes those unfinished are among the most beautiful.

And when something has enriched your life

And when its melody lingers on in your heart

Is it unfinished?

Or is it endless?

~ Viktor Frankl, renowned psychiatrist, author, and Holocaust survivor

Readings for a Suicide

Our friend died at his own battlefield. He was killed in action fighting a civil war. He fought against adversities that were as real to him as his (casket/urn) is real to us. They were powerful adversaries. They took toll of his energies and endurance. They exhausted the last vestiges of his courage and his strength. At last these adversaries overwhelmed him. And it appeared that he had lost the war. But did he? I see a host of victories that he has won!

For one thing he has won our admiration – because even if he lost the war, we give him credit for his bravery on the battlefield. And we give him credit for the courage and pride and hope that he used as his weapons as long as he could. We shall remember not his death, but his daily victories gained through his kindness and thoughtfulness, through his love for his family and friends… for all things beautiful, lovely and honorable. We shall remember not his last day of defeat, but we shall remember the many days that he was victorious over overwhelming odds. We shall remember not the years we thought he had left, but the intensity with which he lived the years that he had.

~ Cendra Lynn, PhD, GriefNet.org

Life is Full of Suffering

Life is full of suffering. To the beloved gathered here has come a grief and loss that strains the ability to bear – to endure the enormity of it and go on.

In the midst of brokenness and broken-heartedness may we know the grace of love that sustains us – love that endures beyond death.

May there be peace and healing. May there be acceptance that NAME, beloved son and husband, father and brother (daughter and wife, and so on) chose his/her healing into death.

May all who must somehow find the courage to continue in the face of the loss of his/her presence receive the grace of healing in life. May we affirm all that was good and true and generous and beautiful in the life of NAME.

May we affirm the love in which he/she was conceived and nurtured and sent forth, an autonomous human being who made his/her own decisions as we all must do. The heart that breaks open can contain the whole world.

Keep breathing. Trust that your heart is large enough.

We are here to mourn the loss and to celebrate the life of NAME.

~ Joanna Macy

Let us speak together. Let us grieve together as we share memories of NAME and all that he/she meant in the lives of those gathered here.

~ Barbara Carlson, Unitarian Universalist minister

My Son... My Son...

Since the beginning of time, people have struggled with the complexities of life, with its mysteries, with its frustrations and injustices, with the ambiguity of "to be or not to be." Since the beginning of time, many cultures have chosen not to speak of self-destruction; to shroud it in silence and to deny it. And, because we as people so often deny death as a part of life, it has enormous power in our lives. I believe, with all my heart, that those things we can bring to light and deal with will lose their destructiveness; and those things which we deny and speak not of claim power in our lives, often destructive power. We must learn that death gives meaning to life so that we can value today and each other and now.

~ Iris Bolton

Poems

Other books and websites include poems about death and loss. We find that most of them are not suitable for reciting to a contemporary audience, as they are not easy to read and follow when read aloud. Often the language is stilted and old fashioned, especially from authors in the 1800s.

You will find a broad selection of poetry at the following websites, among many others:

- FuneralHelper.org/funeral-poetry/non-religious-funeral-poetry.html
- FamilyFriendPoems.com

Quotations

Many people have favorite inspirational quotes that reflect their philosophy of life. Reciting or including a few of the ones that the loved one often shared can be included. Or family members can look through lists of quotes by famous people and find quotes that they think reflected their loved one's point of view and actions. You can enlist several people to read the quotes. Remember to instruct readers as to the pace and volume you'd like them to be recited, so everyone will be able to understand them and microphones will capture it for the recording.

CHAPTER 8

Music

The choice of music varies according to the tone of the service as well as the budget. Set the tone of the service by playing music as guests are arriving. Whether you go the route of recorded or live music, it all enhances the ceremony. You can stimulate or soothe your guests or invoke laughter or tears with the right melody. Consider the mood you want to portray.

Music has a powerful way of bringing us back to important times of remembrance. ("That was the song of our first dance..." or "This was the song Daddy used to always hum..." or "I remember that this was one of Mom's favorite songs to dance to...") In a memorial service, you are likely to feature only two or three songs. Favorite ones can also be included as people gather and perhaps as background if a presentation or video will be shown.

Performers

If the deceased played in a group or with friends, including them in the service adds a personal touch. Make sure the group has the microphone setup they need and that they understand any time constraints. Choose performers who can enhance the service, not detract from it. Make sure you listen to them in advance to avoid surprises.

> ### Imagine...
>
> *The young granddaughter is standing on a riser singing her song about her grandmother. Sharing the microphone is an experienced singer, with a beautiful voice, to accompany her and help her do well...*

Referrals aren't enough. If a non-professional singer is a family member or good friend and asks to perform, perhaps she could play or perform at the reception, sing fewer verses of the song, accompany professionals, or lead a group song or responsive reading. If feathers would be ruffled, sometimes it is worth it to simply let the performance take place. Sometimes a cracked voice is more sincere than the most acclaimed opera singer. After all, we are all family, and we all have talents and flaws.

Music Considerations

Here are some ways to make your music more effective:

- Make sure that background music (as people gather or leave) is soft enough so that people don't have to raise their voices to have a conversation.

- As people enter, play a favorite tune of the deceased or something that celebrated their ethnic or national identity.

- With hymns or secular songs, usually a one- to two-minute version will suffice. Using all seven stanzas of a song can lengthen the service and dampen the mood. Pick the stanzas that have the most meaning for you.

- Religious hymns may be comforting to some and inappropriate to others. Choosing instrumental versions, particularly of religious hymns, is a way to reach a compromise on different belief traditions.

- Upbeat music can work at a service, especially if it is labeled to represent the deceased person's favorite music or her way of looking at the world. We've seen dance music played, and everyone was encouraged to dance because that was reflective of the loved one's personality and desire.

- Sometimes songs can be sung in unison. Asking the group to stand as they sing can also serve as a time to stretch. We were at a religious service where there were obviously different tempos to sing the song among the guests. The minister sang softly because he could not carry a tune. He was not mouthing the words so people could follow his lead. Soon after the start of the five-stanza song, it became apparent that a song leader voice was needed. An experienced song leader is especially beneficial when the song is not well-known by many of the guests.

- Some songs have lyrics that connect us as a community of friends. For this type of song, you might ask people to hold hands as they stand and sing. In a small group, the facilitator might initiate a swaying motion to add a physicality and stronger remembrance to the experience, especially with folk songs.

- Some people have many songs that are important or nostalgic for them or that we remember them by. Each time we hear one of the songs, we conjure up an image or movie in our heads that puts a smile on our face and occasionally a tear. In such a case you might include a list of these songs in the program. This list of songs can also be sent out with thank-you notes. "Remember Bob when you hear these songs that meant so much to him," you might write.

- As with readings, some songs are difficult to comprehend if the words are not clearly pronounced. Add song lyrics to the program or inserted sheet, or change the words for more suitable meaning. If you are using a recorded song, look for a performance where the words are more easily understood.

Although we have stated this before, it is worth repeating here. Rehearsing is a simple precaution that can make a big difference.

Will a CD or other music player be wired into the sound system? Will a microphone need to be placed next to the player? Position the microphone for the best reception. Set up a table and microphone stand in advance. Pay attention to the best volume setting. Assign someone to monitor and adjust the facility's sound system for the best effect.

Technical Aspects of Arranging the Music

Timing has a lot to do with choosing the right music. The stanzas can be too long or too short, and having the right length for selected music can add to the seamlessness of the ceremony. Make it easy to play the right recorded song, or part of a song, at the right time by asking someone who is technically knowledgeable about how to put together musical arrangements. This might make a great volunteer task for a technologically astute teen or young adult.

We have learned the hard way that many people are not good at selecting and playing a particular song from a CD album, especially when using other people's equipment. Even at mortuaries or sanctuaries, the designated sound person may not be there and the new person may have never used the sound system.

Here are some guidelines that simplify the process for everyone: Put CDs in a plain envelope and boldly write on the envelope when the music will be played. Note what the verbal or visual cue will be to push the play button. Example: Processional – Song # 3. Play right after the officiant says, "…and now let us begin our journey of remembrance."

Processional and recessional music is a challenge because most recorded songs are far longer than the time it takes for the participants to walk the length of the space and take their seats. If you must use the entire song, start the music at a low volume; and when the processional begins, increase the music volume to the desired level.

If time allows, have a technically savvy volunteer or paid professional create a CD with just the last segment of a processional or recessional song. Estimate how long it will take for the participants to walk and be seated and have just that amount of the song on the CD. Start the music segment with a two- to three-second volume fade-in and let the song end at its natural fade-out

We recognize that newer forms of music-sharing will always be evolving, so check with the facility or music system provider about what they are experienced in using.

Song Suggestions

Several websites contain an extensive list of songs that refer to death or loss. A web search for "funeral songs" and "songs for funerals" will give you lots of choices. You can begin with fittingfarewell.uk.com.

We carefully reviewed our list of songs for their lyrics, including both the direct and implied meanings. While Beverly leans towards songs with a spiritual or ethereal approach, Dave prefers those that are more secular. The songs labeled with an asterisk * are at Beverly's comfort level, but not Dave's. We have included this information as further evidence that song selection is an individual preference and something that should be discussed among the family members and friends planning a memorial service.

Although we have included the name of a singer next to the song title, there are usually several artists who have recorded the same song. Even with the same title, the song might be different. You can hear most of the versions for free online. Simply search Google or YouTube. When playing recorded songs, find a version where you can best understand the words being sung.

It is also important to not simply go by the title when choosing a song. Read all of the lyrics to ensure the message reflects your sentiment and beliefs. You might want to publish the lyrics you use in the program so they will be easily understood.

Always Look on the Bright Side of Life - Monty Python

Affirmation - Savage Garden

Amazing Grace *

Angel - Sarah McLachlan *

Angel of Love - Cecilia, *Inner Harmony* album *

Angels - Robbie Williams *

Arms Wide Open - Creed

Baby of Mine - Bette Midler

Beautiful Boy - John Lennon

Because You Loved Me - Celine Dion

Borrowed Angels - Kristin Chenoweth *

Bridge Over Troubled Water - Simon and Garfunkel

Bright Eyes - Art Garfunkel

Butterfly Kisses - Bob Carlisle

Circle of Life - Elton John

Come Sail Away - Pirates of the Caribbean

Come Some Rainy Day - Wynona Judd

Everybody Hurts - R.E.M.

Fields of Gold - Eva Cassidy

Fly - Celine Dion *

Forever Young - Rod Stewart

Happy Trails - Roy Rogers and Dale Evans *

I'll Be Seeing You – Michael Bublé

I Will Always Love You - Whitney Houston

I Will Remember You - Sarah McLachlan

I Hope You Dance - Lee Ann Womack

If I Ever Had to Say Goodbye to You - Helen Reddy

I'm Your Child - Barry Manilow

In My Daughter's Eyes - Martina McBride

In My Life - The Beatles

It's a Wonderful World - Louis Armstrong

Let It Be - The Beatles

Longer - Dan Fogelberg *

May It Be - Enya

Memories - Barbara Streisand

My Way - Frank Sinatra

Nothing Compares To You - Sinead O'Connor

On Eagles Wings *

One More Day - Diamond Rio

Over the Rainbow - Judy Garland

Over the Rainbow - Israel Kamakawiwo'ole

Pleasure and Pain - Ben Harper

The Rainbow Connection - Kermit the Frog

Return to Pooh Corner - Kenny Loggins

Seasons in the Sun - Terry Jacks

Simply the Best - Tina Turner

Smile - Rod Stewart

Somewhere Out There - Linda Ronstadt and James Ingram

Spirit in the Sky - Norman Greenbaum

Tears in Heaven - Eric Clapton

Time in a Bottle - Jim Croce

Time to Say Goodbye - Sarah Brightman

To Where You Are - Josh Groban

True Colors - Cyndi Lauper

What a Wonderful World - Israel Kamakawiwo'ole

Unforgettable - Nat King Cole

When the River Meets the Sea - John Denver, performed with
The Muppets

When You're Gone - Avril Lavigne

Who You'd Be Today - Kenny Chesney

You Are So Beautiful - Joe Cocker

You Raise Me Up - Josh Grobin

You'll Never Walk Alone - Gerry and the Peacemakers

You've Got a Friend - James Taylor

Changing a few words can transform a song from spiritual to secular:

"Wind Beneath My Wings" by Bette Midler
(Change last line, just two words, to make it secular.)
Thank God for you, the wind beneath my wings.
I give thanks for you, the wind beneath my wings.

"Who You'd Be Today" by Kenny Chesney
(Change just one word to change the meaning.)
God knows how I miss you.
Nobody knows how I miss you.

Special music may be needed for a miscarriage, stillborn, newborn, or infant. Consider:

Baby Mine - Bette Midler
Angel of Love - Cecilia *

He's Got the Whole World in His Hands *

The Rainbow Connection - Kermit the Frog

This Little Light of Mine

Classical Instrumentals:

Arioso - Bach

Ave Maria - Bach

3rd Symphony Op.55 in E-flat - Beethoven

Raindrop Prelude - Chopin

Piano Sonata No.2 Op.35 in B-flat minor - **Chopin**

Cello Concerto - Elgar

Pavane - Faure

Meditation - Massenet

Laudate Dominum - Mozart

Adagio - Mozart

The Swan - Saint-Saens

Gymnopedie - Satie

Ashoken Farewell - Jay Unger

Winter - Vivaldi

CHAPTER 9

Personalizing Your Service or Ceremony

As mentioned in an earlier chapter, location helps to define the ambiance of the service or ceremony. Adding personal touches will honor the deceased as a unique individual. Go the more traditional route of having flowers or candles, or make your memorial service a true-to-character, zesty, even outrageous celebration of life. Look for support from creative family and friends who would enjoy participating in putting this part of the service together.

Seating

Whenever possible, encourage people to sit closer together rather than in scattered groups. For smaller groups, circles and ovals work well. It can be one large circle or layers of them, with the immediate family in the center ring. Leave some openings for entering and leaving the circle.

If you are in a large sanctuary or a space with fixed seating, there are pros and cons for closing off the back rows that are not likely to be used. By using a cord or ribbon to close off some rows, you make the space more intimate, especially if you don't want to use microphones but do want everyone to be able to hear.

On the other hand, consider that some people are definitely back-row sitters. Those who arrive late or parents with restless children or babies might be less conspicuous in the back. This allows parents to make a hasty exit if needed.

When possible, have the first row of the audience be about six feet from the service participants and, if possible, on the same level or perhaps on a platform to be more easily seen. We've been to auditoriums and social halls where the podium was four feet up. When a six-foot person was speaking to the seated audience, the height difference felt uncomfortably awkward.

> ### Imagine...
>
> *A large sanctuary is made more intimate for a small service, with individual chairs arranged in a semi-circle in front of the pews, so that guests can feel more connected to the ceremony. A small low table holds ceremonial items.*

Memorabilia

Consider a table filled with pictures and memorabilia. Some attendees may only know a small portion of the life of the deceased, so this is a good way to paint a broader picture. Here are some suggestions:

- Use items that tell a story. Newspaper articles or letters of commendation? Group pictures from vacations? Hockey fanatic? Master gardener? If space and logistics allow you can include things like a surfboard, saddle, or motorcycle.

- Ask guests to leave pictures and mementos for the family. Make sure to mention this well in advance so guests will have time to gather their items to bring. Label items for significance (e.g., "The Green and Johnson Families, Adirondacks circa 1972"). These items can later be gifted to the family and compiled in the book. Or guests may decide to take them home after the gathering. Friends and relatives will likely have interesting pictures that you and others have never seen.

- Children can draw pictures of their recollections of their grandpa to be displayed at the reception.

- Create a video slideshow of pictures. The show can be running as people enter the lobby before the service or at the reception. This requires forethought, so gather pictures well in advance. You might want to assign this project to a tech-savvy teen to help get them involved in their family history. For a slideshow of pictures, consider adding descriptive titles, sharing details like who, what, where, and when.

Balloons

If you are aiming for a light-hearted party atmosphere, most attendees will get the idea and join in. You might want to use the favorite colors of the deceased or even colors of their favorite sports team. Less expensive, thinner balloons lose their helium more quickly and thus can't be inflated hours ahead of time and still look perky. Do a pre-test to make sure they will last through the ceremony.

Consider the consequences of releasing helium-filled, Mylar, or latex balloons with ribbons. This often presents a problem for people and animals. Balloons can drift long distances and litter populated areas or affect wildlife habitats where they are a danger to animals. Find out more at BalloonsBlow.org.

Imagine...

Consider what can happen to balloons without proper care and attention. A deflated balloon attached to a string falls into a pond as a hazard to fish and fowl. An old balloon gets stuck in a high tree. A bunch of balloons skitter through traffic and distract drivers...

Candle Lighting

Family members could light a candle for a time of remembrance. Check with the facility regarding candle use. Many do not allow handheld candles due to damage from dripping wax.

Candle Lighting and Extinguishing Ceremony

Begin with an unlit candle.

"Today, we honor our (beloved) (mother) and friend, NAME. I light this candle to symbolize how we hold NAME in our community memory. Let us be inspired by her memory to carry on her good work and share the stories of her impact on our community to inspire others.

We can no longer share the touch of her hand, the sound of her voice, or the sight of her beautiful smile. I extinguish this flame to symbolize her physical death. Yet, the memories of NAME, her (special character), and her (gifts) live on in our lives. Her (wonderful spirit) is carried within us."

Unique Processionals

A Sparkler Processional

An outside evening processional could be with firework sparklers. Each person can have two sticks. One person lights the first sparkler, which is used to light the second stick, and so on. You might want to experiment with a trial run to make sure the timing is what you want and expect. Keep in mind that some states do not allow fireworks to be shipped into their state.

Imagine...

As the casket or urn is transported to the front of the group, garden club members form an arch, with their long-handled gardening tools in salute of their loved one...

Special Interest Honor Guard

Was the person in a special interest group with identifiable clothing or objects? A TV show profiled a close group of chainsaw wood carvers. At a wedding of one of their friends, thirty woodcarvers formed parallel lines of roaring chainsaws, held in the air, as the couple left the ceremony. A similar activity could take place for your loved one if they are closely identified with a particular item that they use in a group.

Decorations around a Particular Interest

Cheese head? Hydrangea Society? Quilter? Car-racing fanatic? Sports enthusiast? You get the idea. Individuals or groups can bring specialty items to be used to decorate the reception gathering room.

> ### Imagine...
>
> *A two-foot wide by six-foot long piece of butcher paper spread across a table in the reception room. At sequential places along a drawn line are dates significant to the loved one's life events. Pens or markers are provided for guests to write their names and a thought or memory next to the events they shared with the person who has died*

Timelines Tell a Story and Get People Involved

Create a timeline of the deceased's life on a long piece of heavy butcher paper or the backside of a roll of wallpaper or giftwrap. Post your timeline on a wall. Use a felt-tip marker to place date-ranges of life milestones, such as birth, high school, college, marriage, birth of children and grandchildren, or retirement. The guests can use markers to add their names around the dates of a shared experience (volunteer activity, thoughtful gesture, odd job, travel adventure, or even a bit of mischief as a child).

> ### Imagine...
>
> *A computer-created family tree, enlarged by a sign and banner service, is attached to a wall at the reception so folks can find out how people are related. Pens or markers are available for filling in missing names and date*

A few guidelines:

If using a wall, check to see what methods of attachment are permitted; or simply use a long table.

- Make sure the markers don't bleed through the paper and mark the table or wall. Consider using crayons.

- Leave room on the top and bottom of the timeline for guest comments.

- Give people the idea of what you want them to do by adding examples in advance.

- Let teens encourage folks to participate, hand out markers, and provide suggestions. Some guests may have poor handwriting or disabilities and the teens can assist by doing the writing.

Family Tree

A large tree drawing is helpful with a large family gathering. Displayed on the wall of the reception area, it lets family members connect and helps them to explain their relationships to the children. We recommend creating one well in advance and using your gathering to help fill in the missing names and dates that some family members may remember.

Check the facility rules before attaching anything to a wall, and allow plenty of time to create the tree. You may need to try a couple of prototypes before you have one nice enough to show in public. Add pictures when possible.

Ask family members to bring names and dates from their branch of the family. Some relatives may have already created their own family tree, which can be incorporated within the large drawing. This is a valuable task to assign to a creative volunteer, perhaps a young family member interested in family history.

There are many free online template-software programs to help organize the information. You can email the file to a banner-printing service to make it any size you like, using either paper or vinyl. Compare prices. Large commercial printers can be a source of large sheets of heavy paper. Go to the loading platform and ask to talk to a production supervisor. They often have stacks of one-sided misprints that they scrap.

Flowers and Plants

There are many opinions to consider regarding the use of flowers at services and ceremonies. If possible, let people know about family wishes in advance. Did the deceased have a favorite plant or a reputation for growing particular flowers? Do you want friends to bring flowers? Do you want a color theme? What will be done with flowers after the service?

If a floral spray is designed particularly for a funeral, its use is limited unless you disassemble the flowers for smaller arrangements. If there are more casual displays, the family or friends could be invited to take home a flower or an arrangement. Bring containers and stem cutters to rearrange and transport the flowers.

You can also donate floral arrangements to an elder-care facility or hospital. Check in advance with the facility to make sure they are wanted. Make preparations in advance for someone to bring a suitable vehicle to transport them.

Live plants may be used instead of cut flowers. Perhaps they can be brought from the deceased's or a friend's garden. Bring them in decorative or wrapped containers. The plants can later be put into a community, congregational, or memorial garden space. Make careful arrangements for the plants, especially in hot and dry months. Plan ahead to supply a durable sign that includes the name of the person and any other pertinent information that could be posted near the plant.

Plants are available for rent in many areas with conference and convention centers. Companies that rent potted indoor plants in decorative containers for events typically offer delivery and pickup services as well. Search plant rentals on the Internet. Local garden nurseries may also rent plants, if you ask them. Pick an amount you are willing to spend, and ask them what they would be willing to do for that amount of money. They may also provide delivery service since they already have the trucks and carts.

A memorial tree provides a lasting tribute. Plant a sapling tree or have a larger tree planted in an easily accessed and visible location. You might also consider having a tree planted in the person's honor, perhaps through a reforestation project. In Atlanta, Georgia, there is a nonprofit urban forestation organization called Trees Atlanta that funds tree planting along city streets. Find related organizations around the world through an online search.

Tree transplanting services can move a tree large enough to provide shade. Cost factors are tree size, distance to transport, and access to the dig and planting sites. You could even buy a sapling Japanese Maple, many years in advance of need, for your own garden. This could be moved to a public or congregational spot when the day comes. Plant it in a large container to make it easier to move. Bring a picture of the tree you planted in your loved one's honor to the memorial service.

Contributions in Lieu of Flowers

If you request a donation in lieu of flowers, make it easy for guests to donate in advance or at the service. You may want to invite a representative of the charity to the service to let guests know how the money will be used. That person might also be at the reception to receive donations. Most charities have mobile devices to accept credit cards remotely, so donations can be made immediately.

Contributing to a specific purpose rather than a general fund will encourage more people to participate. For instance, you may be contributing to a bench at the botanical garden in honor of the deceased. Some people use the occasion to start a charitable fund or foundation in honor of the person. Starting from scratch requires extensive effort and paperwork. It is easier to find a related charity and create a fund for your loved one under that umbrella organization.

Butterfly Release

Butterflies are usually sent in the cocoon phase and are timed to hatch just before you want to release them. There may be weather and seasonal constraints to consider. Search the web to find suppliers and become educated about the process.

Dove Release

A white dove release ceremony can be a lasting memory, especially when words seem inadequate. Releasing a living creature has a physical as well as a spiritual impact. Instead of a 21 Gun Salute, many bird services offer a 21 Dove Salute. As everyone watches the doves circle overhead, the magical moment happens as they all disappear into the distance. Ask a professional how to make your ceremony even more meaningful and memorable. These trained birds must be able to make their way back home after the ceremony; as such there are limitations on the distance and conditions under which the birds will travel.

The National White Dove Release Society is a good place to start your search in the US. Go to NWDRS.net to find services listed in other countries. (WhiteDoveSociety.org)

Fun and Unifying Clothing or Hats

Is there a favorite color, style of dress, or period costume that your loved one was famous for wearing? Lots of folks in attendance wearing a similar style of clothing can show solidarity.

Imagine...

A remembrance ceremony where the ladies of the Fancy Hat Club are all wearing their favorite hats while the hat of their beloved friend rests on an empty chair

Mementos for Guests to Take Home

If guests travel from great distances and you plan to give a memento, choose one that travels well in a suitcase, such as a card with embedded flower seeds (children could paste these together in advance of your ceremony). Other options to consider: a picture booklet with favorite recipes or flower bulbs from your or the deceased individual's garden. If the loved one was a collector, this might be a good time to give away those ball caps, CDs and records, neckties, costume jewelry, or refrigerator magnets.

Memory Notes

Volunteers at the guestbook table can encourage guests to fill out a memory note. This is a 3x5 index card with a sentimental phrase like "I'll always remember when…" or "A fond memory of you is…" Have pens and a writing space available. Ask for contact information, such as name and relationship to the deceased, for the family's future reference.

You can order preprinted cards through websites like NextGenMemorials.com in the US or MemorialKeepsakes.com.au in Australia.

Nametags

Nametags are helpful for any occasion. While we don't see them often used in a memorial service, they are valuable in helping neighbors, co-workers, and other guests connect with each other, and are especially helpful to relatives of the deceased. Families who haven't been together in a long time may not recognize each other or their growing children.

Use prewritten tags for family and people you are confident will attend and blank ones for others. Place them on an easily accessible table with an upright sign. Provide pointed felt-tip pens and markers so the tags can be easily read. Be sure to have a trash receptacle or container for throwing away the backs of the nametags.

Assisting with nametags is a great job for a teenaged relative. The task will keep them busy and interacting with guests at the memorial service. They will likely assist by writing names on the tags, so check in advance to see if they can write neatly.

Here are some examples for nametags:

Tom Miller
Grandson

Li Wong
Best Friend of 35 years

Joe Lipton
Garden Club

Juan Martinez
Co-worker at IBM

Susie Chapman
High school baseball team

One alternative for a small family is to have a person introduce the family members to other guests before the ceremony begins.

Many of the guests will likely be there to support one of the family members and will not know the other relatives.

CHAPTER 10

Receptions

A reception is the time to greet one another, remember the loved one, catch up with family or friends we don't see often, and have something to eat. Mourning and attending a service requires a lot of emotional energy. We need food and drink to keep our spirits from flagging even more.

You may wish to let other people assist the family by contributing food or drink to the event. Friends can also set up and run the reception. Many of us know people who thrive with this kind of service. Such individuals are often well-organized, nurturing, and knowledgeable about how to serve lots of people at once. There may be a person who loves logistics and decorations or handling food and cleanup. Be sure to involve them as you are planning a memorial service and reception for your loved one.

Considerations when Planning the Reception

- How many attendees?
- Will most be standing or sitting? (This may depend on the age and ability of those who attended the memorial service.)

- What tone do you want to set?

- Do you want to maintain a solemn atmosphere through the reception? Or is it time to lighten up the mood, perhaps with the sing-along group the deceased belonged to for 30 years?

- How long do you anticipate people staying?

- Are there enough plates, forks, cups, and napkins? Where are the trashcans and trash bags?

- Do you want to include a table with pictures and mementos of the loved one? You may need to arrange to have someone move them from the memorial service space.

- Do you really want to serve alcohol? This decision could be asking for trouble. The sad can get sadder at a funeral, or those with a grudge against a family member may get belligerent. Consider who will be coming to your memorial service prior to making a decision on alcohol.

- A pianist, singer, or group of musicians, who may have been not-so-appropriate to enlist for the service, can add just the right touch as family and friends make the transition from mourning back into the real world during an after-service reception. Keep the music volume low enough for conversation to be heard.

- The reception is a good opportunity for people to share their anecdotes about the deceased in a more relaxed, less formal environment. Arrange in advance for someone to be the master of ceremonies.

- Do you need a sound system for music or shared remembrances?

- In a congregation, a care committee may take over the providing and serving of food.

- A catered event eases the burden on the family if it fits within your budget.

- Small groups may choose to meet at a restaurant to rest, relax, and remember after the taxing ceremony. Chinese restaurants usually have large round tables that make it easier to talk to everyone at the table.

- There may be more people who wish to share remembrances than time could be allotted for at the ceremony. Arrange for a microphone to be available at your reception or gathering after the service. If you had the service recorded, record this portion as well. It may well have significance for the family for years to come.

- If the reception is going to be held in a home, see our "Using Volunteers" section so that it can be run more smoothly.

CHAPTER 11
Recording the Service and/or Reception

You only have one opportunity to record your memorial service or reception. Not recording a memorial service is like not having a photographer or videographer at a wedding. The emotional stress on the family dramatically reduces their memory of what happens. Family and dear friends who could not attend always appreciate seeing and hearing what was said and done. Having a DVD of the service is a wonderful addition to the family archives.

Check with the congregation or funeral home to be certain that videotaping of the service is allowed. If possible, have an experienced videographer check the details so there aren't any glitches. For the editing, determine in advance which parts of the service are most important to capture. Taping someone walking up to the microphone can make the DVD too long, which adds to editing time or expense. In addition, you may not wish to record the entire length of every song or silent meditation.

Recording Guidelines to Consider

The videographer will need to consider the location of the power outlets, the direction of the light, program content, and seating arrangements in order to plan ahead. The camera will likely need to be mounted on a six-foot-high tripod for better shots when the audience is standing.

Proper microphone placement is vital. If you set up a microphone on a stand for sharing, assign someone to stand next to it and adjust the height and position of the microphone for each speaker. Poor microphone use and problems that occur when individuals think they don't need to use a microphone make the service less pleasant for those in attendance, and can also prevent capturing important sharing at your service.

Plug the camera into a facility sound system whenever possible. Microphones built into the camera often result in poor sound quality or produce an echo effect when video is shot indoors. Attaching the videographer's wireless microphones to the house microphone stands also helps with the recorded sound.

Because people sharing from the audience are rarely heard well, whenever possible, ask audience members to come to the front of the room to share through the main microphone. Large congregations now have listening systems for those with hearing problems. Let the audience know if this service is available, and have someone assist those who may need such a service.

If a child or teenager is speaking, have someone hold the microphone in the correct position. Consider a stepstool for children to reach the microphone and be seen by the videographer and the audience. Because funerals can be traumatic for children, decide in advance if the child has the maturity and desire to participate in this way.

If you decide to have remembrance sharing during the reception, make sure the videographer knows in advance so the gear can be quickly shifted to a new location and the microphone will be readjusted.

Broadcasting the Service via the Internet

Live streaming, sharing the service on the Internet, is relatively easy for a professional with the proper equipment. It allows anyone with Internet access, anywhere in the world, to see the service as it is happening. Funeral homes are increasingly offering this service, and there are independent services you may be able to hire.

Video sharing and conferencing services, such as Skype, allow people in other parts of the country or the world to participate with a live message, testimonial, or eulogy. This can be quite complicated, so consult with a professional to make sure it is done correctly and smoothly at the service.

CHAPTER 12

Logistics

Plan the service details to avoid unnecessary problems. Without proper planning of logistical details, you may hear comments such as:

- I couldn't find a place to park.

- It was so hot I couldn't breathe.

- I couldn't hear a word that was said.

- The music was too long.

- That great uncle just kept going on and on.

- I never got a program.

- Was there a guestbook?

Before the Service

Assessing who is coming will help reduce the stress of the day. Here are some questions to ask when planning the service:

If the service is taking place outside, what is your Plan B if weather changes and it rains or snows?

Are there considerations for disabled or elderly attendees? Consider those who have trouble walking or who are in a wheelchair. How will they move across the choppy meadow to the pond? Avoid potential upsets. Perhaps one service can be held at the retirement home, with another held at the beach.

Are chairs provided for those who need to sit?

Do the hearing-impaired need seating close to the sound system, podium, or speaker?

How many people are expected?

Where will guests park?

Is signage needed? Who will create it?

If using programs, how many will be printed? How will they be distributed?

Is there someone designated to take care of restless kids during and after the service?

During the Service

- Will anyone need to lie down during the service or be taken home early?

- How many family members, close friends, or dignitaries will attend? Where will they sit?

- How will the chairs be placed? Chairs can be arranged in an open curve if there is a podium or stage. Use a circular, oval, or open curve for smaller, more intimate gatherings.

When using a space with more seating than the number of people expected, block off the rear area to encourage more intimate seating in the front. If you know there will be babies or toddlers, have ushers assist the family to the rear aisle seats for a potential easy and non-disruptive exit.

- Will guests be able to see everyone who will be speaking?

- Do you have access to the thermostat? Do you know how to change the temperature inside the building if necessary?

- Do you need a sound system or microphones? If so, have someone designated to handle the sound levels and any related issues. Consider having an additional microphone in the front of the space so people can be heard and seen without getting on and off the podium. Have someone available to adjust the microphone position.

- If using a podium, will a stepstool or riser box be needed for shorter participants to easily reach the microphone and be seen over the podium?

- If a guestbook will be available, where will it be? Who will encourage guests to sign it? Ask them to include their connection to the family or the deceased. What kind of pens will you use?

- Will nametags be available? If so, encourage each person to write their relationship to the deceased. Use a sharp-pointed, felt-tip marker for easier reading.

- Will the service or reception be videotaped? Allow time for the videographer to set up.

- Are flowers expected? Where will they be placed?

- Will you distribute tissues for mourners? Who will do this and when?

- Where will you place the memorial table with pictures and mementos?

- Who will set up the reception and when? Who will clean up?

After the Service

- Do all in attendance have the address of the reception and directions to the gravesite or other gathering?

- Will there be a car processional to the site? If so, who will lead it?

- Is there adequate and safe parking?

While this appears to be a long list of details to consider, keep in mind you don't have to do it alone. Recruit willing volunteers who don't have an official role in the program to assist with key areas.

CHAPTER 13
"What Can I Do to Help?"
Using Volunteers

Delegating Before, During
and After the Service

You can't do everything yourself and others want to help, so give them that opportunity and make it easier on yourself. After all, you are giving a gift to others when you permit them to give a gift of service to you. You may be reluctant to ask for help, but for many people it is an honor to participate. They may genuinely prefer to do something useful rather than simply sit around.

Recruit a home guardian and other trusted backups. Who is going to guard the family possessions?

When one man's mother died, as her children were starting to straighten up and distribute her belongings, distant relatives opened the door, walked in, and started to pick up and pack belongings they claimed were rightfully theirs. The immediate family was too stunned to object, but this incident created a family chasm that is still difficult to cross.

If the reception after the service is in the home of the deceased, some visitors have been known to rifle through the jewelry box or linen closet. Valuable or sentimental items can disappear. Limit access to parts of the house you consider to be private.

Assign a Volunteer Coordinator

Create a detailed volunteer checklist. Keep track of the jobs that need to be done, and who has committed to performing specific duties. Make sure that the volunteer has the skill and time to do the task. If possible, have at least one person as a support, because most tasks are more enjoyable when shared with others. Have a backup to fill in for emergencies.

Many of the assignments and responsibilities will begin days before the actual service. Some require ordering of products or services, advance notice, setup, coordination with others, or rehearsal.

Below is a list of sample volunteer activities. If you create a computerized chart, use the landscape rather than portrait layout. Of course, these are guidelines. You will want to choose volunteer activities that can be used in your situation.

List of Volunteer Opportunities

To help you remember the tasks and who will do them we suggest that you create a multi-column list such as the one below:

Task	Name	Contact info	Due date
Pick up flowers	*Jane Doe*	*Janedoe27@email.com* *777-9311*	*10/28*
Call guests	*John Doe*	*Johndoe27@email.com* *470-9311*	*11/1*

Notices

- Write and submit obituary
- Assemble lists of people and organizations to notify
- Organize sympathy cards with return addresses (kept for envelopes for thank-you notes)

Transportation

- Handle visitor trips from and to the airport or hotel
- Trips to and from the ceremonies for visitors
- Pick up and return food, flowers, and rented items

Care

- Babysitting or pet-sitting services

Reception

- Arrange for microphone and room setup

- Set up canopy to protect from sun or rain

- Coordinate food and drink, including tables, decorations, tableware, and serving pieces

- Leftover food – packing and distributing

- Someone to bring needed containers for leftover food

- Coordinate cleanup

- Pay service providers

Parking

- Assist in directing parking

- Design and display signage

> ### Imagine...
>
> *A neighbor cleaning up the yard of the family home before family and friends gather after the service or stay for a few days in grief support...*

Preparing for Visitors

- Clean the family home before and after the events

- Help young children get dressed and take them to the toilet

- Shop for groceries

- Wash the windows

- Wash the car

- Do the laundry

- Small repairs

- Provide a full-course, home-cooked meal (instead of one more cake)

- Shovel the snow

- Buy stamps at the post office

- Water the potted plants

- Help sort the items left behind by the deceased

- Provide rides to and from appointments, soccer practice, and dance lessons

- Find out about other obligations that need to be fulfilled and see how you can help (the mother with Alzheimer's, the pet to the vet, invitations to be mailed for the daughter's upcoming wedding)

Family Activities

Plan and coordinate family story-sharing and recording when family is together before or after services.

CHAPTER 14
Dealing with Family Tensions

Material for this topic is summarized, and expanded from the 2nd edition of *Remembering Well: Rituals for Celebrating Life and Mourning Death* by Sarah York. The book is required reading for many celebrant training and thanatology programs around the world. We highly recommend it. Since we are not experts on this topic, we are sharing Sarah York's insight, with her permission.

When there are hurt feelings between family members or upset relationships with the deceased, creating a healing service or a meaningful time together becomes more complicated. *At no time are we more aware of our familial flaws than when a family member dies.* It is important to find ways to acknowledge the grief that is wrapped in ongoing alienation and broken relationships.

Ritual expression cannot heal or erase the wounds of a broken relationship, but it can help people face up to and identify the nature of their pain. There are some basic principles for calming the waters if family members are estranged or upset:

- Gathering in a group can have a calming influence and is an invitation to call a timeout or truce.

- Include people who are not involved in conflicts and hurt feelings to help reduce the chances for inappropriate outbursts and heated emotions.

- Service officiants should be neutral. They should not be identified with either side of any dispute, so that the thoughts of the service are directed toward the person who has died rather than any underlying feelings of hurt or animosity.

- The ceremony location should be neutral to create a sacred space for everyone. If that is not possible, consider creating a second service for those on the other side of the fence if it is needed, desired, or appropriate.

- Don't expect to totally satisfy everyone in attendance, including yourself. Some compromises are inevitable.

- A neutral coordinator could provide suggestions to those who will be sharing a eulogy or testimonial. If someone tries to "wing it" and talk extemporaneously, this could open the door for speakers to say something inappropriate or upsetting, and time limits could be ignored. What we say and how we say it is sometimes not what people hear and feel. Ask speakers to forward a copy of their message to a coordinator. Asking for notes in advance also will also give the officiant an idea of how long each person intends to speak.

Family "secrets" carry an amazing power to create and maintain unhealthy divisions and alliances within families and the friends who support each side. Secrets can include:

1. trauma or abuse of one person against another
2. a small circle of people who may know about someone's "troubled past"
3. hurtful or very private information that was told in confidence and is about to be blabbed to the world
4. the thing that most everyone know about but nobody talks about, the unmentionable (such as addiction or abuse)

Whatever family secret is at play, the effects are the same: honest communication is compromised. Sometimes people will keep secrets to protect others from being hurt, but their dishonesty creates barriers. Secrets are often more hurtful concealed than when revealed.

Inheritance issues have a uniquely powerful tendency to create or increase hurt feelings. This often happens when multiple relationships, marriages, and children from different partners are a part of the equation. Seldom do all parties feel the division of dollars or property is fair or reasonable.

Financial issues can foster jealousy and upsets. Feelings of worth / lack of worth, acceptance / non-acceptance, validation / invalidation and reward / punishment are a just a few of the emotions that take on new and powerful meaning when a death occurs. Many of these people may have a challenge in being nice to each other at the funeral or memorial service.

Are there quick fixes to these emotions? No. Do you need to vent and share all of your feelings at the funeral? No. Can you just be polite? That would be a good thing. Is it valuable to be aware of these feelings when planning what is done and said before, during, and after the service? Yes.

The service is a unique time to open doors of communication, healing, and understanding. One common slight occurs when stepparents, stepchildren, ex-spouses, same-sex partners, or other significant relatives are not acknowledged with special seating or recognition at the service or in the obituary.

Missed opportunities for acceptance, or at least mending fences, is a repeating theme that Sarah has heard during the span of her career. Don't let this opportunity pass you by. This is a unique window of time when acceptance and reconciliation are possible, as people may be reconsidering their priorities.

If you can't get the family together due to hard feelings, professional guidance could at least help you improve the dynamics of your family. Consider hiring an experienced family therapist to help mediate conversations that may lead to some kind of healing compromise or understanding. You'll be very glad you did for years and perhaps generations to come. (Read more about Sarah York and her books at SarahYork.com.)

When Family and Friends Can't
or Won't Come Together

There are a variety of reasons memorial services or public gatherings may not materialize. Families are sometimes faced with a situation where loved ones don't want any service at the end of life. Often, people who are near the end of their lives don't want to be burdened with the idea of what will happen after they are gone. In other cases, they simply don't want their loved ones to be burdened with the expense and responsibility of creating a memorial service. In other cases, money or other obligations may prevent families from coming together.

Other difficult situations may result in the decision not to plan a memorial service. There may be a deceased person where this description applies:

The schizophrenic brother

The severely mentally-ill

The person who abandoned the family

The person with a history of emotional or physical abuse

The mean aunt who criticized everyone and everything

The brother who was estranged from the family

There is no getting around the fact that situations like these are difficult to reconcile. When funerals and services can bring out the dysfunction in many families, it may be best to simply have a small service or ceremony that will provide at least some kind of closure for the family. In such cases, consider asking someone to share a story about the person from a positive perspective: "What I learned from Don…" or "How Sheila taught me a valuable lesson about life…"

This is not a time to belittle or gang up on someone who is not present; nor is it a time to sugarcoat the difficulties that this person went through or put others through. Perhaps this is a time when someone would choose to forgive the person publicly for all the pain that had been created; perhaps not. You might choose to end the service with a toast to "what might have been."

Whatever the tone of the service, it is important that one leader make the decision as to how the service will unfold in advance. The goal is to create closure, not to open wounds that will continue to exude pain for years to come. Find additional guidelines for grieving difficult people at the website OpenToHope.com.

The "No-Travel" Ceremony

This may hit the spot with some families and friends. Everyone can stay where they are while paying homage to the one they have lost. Here are some possibilities for a memorial service that does not require travel to a distant location:

- Hold a gathering on Skype or other video conversation / sharing sites, where family members from anywhere in the world can call in to share their thoughts and feelings of the one they have lost. Go to TimeAndDate.com/world clock to ensure that everyone knows when the gathering will begin and end. One person should be the organizer and keep things flowing. This is a good time to share remembrances or favorite readings.

- Create a compilation CD or DVD of photos, video, or music that can be posted on YouTube, Vimeo, or one of many tribute websites. There are memorial tribute websites, some even offered by mortuaries or funeral homes, that enable families to post biographical information about their loved one and share their remembrances. Search for "memorial tributes websites" for an extensive list.

- Have a dinner party. Plan for everyone (wherever they are) to eat Uncle Bob's favorite food on Friday night. (Pepperoni pizza? Chocolate chip cookies?)

- Buy fresh flowers or find a picture of Aunt Clara's favorite flower.

- Watch a favorite movie that can be accessed via website or viewed on Netflix.

- Send a CD of favorite music selections to be listened to at the same time.

- Share remembrances that loved ones have written, either by mail or e-mail.

- Consider having each of the participants do the same things at the same time or at least on the same day. Although this certainly isn't required, it's a bit more meaningful if you know that other friends and relatives are honoring your loved one in the same way and at the same time.

CHAPTER 15

Involving Children

When adults are busy going through their own grieving process, it is all too easy to forget that the younger ones are grieving, too. From toddlers to teens, it is important to make sure their feelings and reactions don't fall through the cracks. When we don't know what to say to a grieving child, we tend not to say anything, losing the opportunity to connect with and support the child.

Children who have had experiences with dying pets or wild animals that have died are better equipped to understand death in people. Creating a formalized burial ceremony for a pet, even the dead squirrel in the road, creates a time for conversation about death, loss, and mourning.

There are many books, websites, and support groups around how children and teens handle grief. Start with books and YouTube talks by Earl Grollman.

What to Say and Do Around
the Death Experience

To help things go as smoothly as possible, here are some things to think about, especially when you are dealing with younger children or those who were especially close to the one who is gone. Listen to what the child is saying to find out how much he has absorbed and how much pain he is feeling. There are many books and articles on the Internet that deal with children, loss, and grief. Refer to them for any specific issues. In the meantime, below are some thoughts to consider.

Many children, like adults, have a fear of death, especially the death of a loved one. If your child prefers not to talk about the death, know that there are still emotions at play beneath the surface. There is no set timetable for grief. Make sure the child understands what will happen during the burial or cremation process before he is confronted with the containers at the service.

Before the memorial service, be sure the child knows what to expect. Prepare the child for the likelihood that people may cry and be sad. Help them know that there may be lots of pictures of Grandpa, but Grandpa won't be there. You may choose to explain that Grandpa's ashes are in the urn. Explain the different parts of the service.

If there is an open casket, prepare the child for what he might expect to see. This can be especially traumatic, so do not force the child to do what he doesn't want to do. Coach children, in advance, about appropriate things to say when they interact with kids or adults.

"No" means "no." Do not force a child to attend or participate, and don't guilt him into it. Have a backup plan for what to do. Let the child know in advance who will be caring for him if he has to leave, and be prepared with activity materials, snacks, and knowledge of bathroom locations. Through all levels of maturity and understanding and across the many situations involving death and remembrance, one of the best ways to help children is to get them involved.

How Children Can Participate

Some of these suggestions have been covered in other chapters, but they bear repeating in this list:

- Invite related children to share a remembrance at the appropriate time. Let them practice what they are going to say so they will feel more comfortable when the time comes to talk. Have a microphone adjusted for their height or have something for them to stand on to reach the microphone. Show them how to use the microphone properly.
- Depending on their age and maturity, each can give their name and relationship to the deceased or the oldest can

introduce each member of a group. Each one can share just one or two things they loved or remember about the deceased. It may be a good idea to have them bring something to read that an adult helped them to write.

Imagine...

A group of children and adults using colored fabric markers to draw or write messages of love, admiration, and appreciation on a rectangular piece of white material, possibly even weeks in advance of a death. Spreading out that "Love Flag" on top of the closed casket, like an American flag in a veteran's burial service. The flag is then folded into a triangular shape and presented to members of the family as a keepsake...

- Staff a welcome table with older kids who know most of the family.

- A "Love Flag" can be created and used in a memorial service where there is a casket or has been a cremation. When the Love Flag has been put into the display case, there will be space behind it to store the remains in a decorative bag. In order to have the flag fold up into a triangle and fit properly into a standard display case, the fabric should be cut into a 32-inch by 68-inch size. See our website for other details.

- In a home funeral situation, or when a fiberboard or plain wooden box is made by friends or purchased in advance, children and adults can write and draw directly on the casket as a part of a more intimate service by a small group.

- Usher guests to their seats.

- Decorate the ceremonial space.

- Sit with and support younger children.

- Where appropriate, have a child sit with an elderly family member, holding her hand for emotional support.

- Share a reading or remembrance as a group, each reading or remembering a small part. Practice and have a plan to assist or take over if emotions require it. (You may be tempted to jump in right away to rescue the child from embarrassment, but it may simply help to give them a few minutes to regain their composure and move on.)

- Have an older child or teen read or share a remembrance independently.

- Discuss in advance what the child would like for you to do if they become overwhelmed with emotion. You could also have the child write what they would like to share and have someone else read it while standing next to them.

- Help with the reception and food setup.

- Play an instrument or sing as part of a group.

- Help direct car parking before the service.

- Individually, or as a group, have children and teens create a display board that can include notes, poems, family pictures, artwork, or memorabilia.

- Help select what the deceased will wear in the casket.

- Help select the music for the service.

- Pass out tissues before the service starts.

CHAPTER 16

Special Circumstances: Tragic or Unexpected Deaths

This is an uncomfortable part of the book to write, and there is nothing that we can suggest that is an easy formula for getting through this difficult time. We are talking about the most emotional circumstances surrounding a death, such as murder, suicide, accidents from fire, drowning, teen-driving accidents, overdose, natural disaster, or even a hero's death. Death of a stillborn, newborn, infant, young child, or teen fits into a whole different category of grief.

There is no glazing over these issues. They are tough to handle, and there are usually many questions surrounding the situation that begin with the word, "Why?"

Sometimes, when the pain is terribly difficult, the only thing we can do is keep moving, one step at a time, especially since we can only let the actuality of the loss seep in one brainwave at a time. Crying can be a big part of the entire grieving process, and it is also acceptable for the ones closest to the one who has died to exhibit little or no emotion. They just aren't there yet.

Many of us have experienced deep, bottomless sadness where we don't dare let go. It's like the heart is a helium balloon. Once the air starts to burst out, it seems there will be nothing left in the end. Sometimes the best we can do is to hold on, without any hint of emotion. Know this: the emotion will come in its own time.

So while your ears are ringing, your body is numb, and tears are spilling over or just won't come, the whole world appears to be going on without you. Family and friends need extra reassurance that you just can't seem to give. When you find yourself in such a situation, *stop*. Don't try to be the hero. Take a breath and repeat as much as you need to and repeat to yourself, "I'm doing the best I can."

One of the best sites we have found for moving through grief is OpenToHope.com, sponsored by Dr. Gloria Horsley and her daughter, Dr. Heidi Horsley. You may find that one of their radio or TV shows or articles will help you through your personal process. We have provided more helpful resources on our website, HeartfeltMemorialServices.com.

Suicide

The words and songs you decide to use are dependent on how the family feels. They may want to avoid mentioning any reference of suicide. For instance, a grandfather may have been told that the death of his grandson came from a health issue because the family wanted to protect the grandfather and his own fragile state.

If the family does want to make the suicide an open subject, use your discretion about how and when to refer to it. You might decide to set a tone of remembering the best about the person, regardless of the circumstances that led you to today.

If your loved one was chronically ill and opted out of longer suffering, you could refer to his courage to live.

If a young person "in the prime of her life" has died, it is more difficult to find things to say. You might choose to focus on her sensitivity to so many aspects of life, making it impossible for her to function and fit into today's world.

You might also want to concentrate most on the family and friends who tried their best to love and support the one who committed suicide – they may be suffering because they were not able to prevent it from happening.

CHAPTER 17
Small or Special Ceremonies

Sometimes a small group of family and friends prefers a more private, intimate ceremony. You may decide to hold a service in someone's backyard, by a brook, or in a living room. Define the space as a special area, using a rug, plants, or other items that set the space apart.

Here are some items you could include:

- Tablecloth in a favorite color, design, or style

- Candle (remember lighter / matches)

- Suitable candle holder for use outdoors if there is a breeze

- Pictures of the loved one with family members

- Snack or favorite food to share

- Drink for a toast along with cups or glasses

- Vase of flowers

- Favorite song or type of music

- Sheet music or lyrics for singing together

- Reading, meditation, or prayer for people to hear or recite

- Box of tissues for tears

- Clothing that is nostalgic, unique, or fun

- For kids, fun hats from craft paper

- Balloons

Ceremony Sequence of Events

- Choose someone to lead the ceremony.

- Ask people to turn off phones.

- Give a welcoming as you light a candle.

- Play a recording or sing a song together.

- Share a food item story.

  (e.g., "Grandma made these cookies with me every time we went to visit.")

- Begin "I remember" sharing.

- Have a moment of silent reflection or prayer.

- Lift a toast to the beloved.

- Play or sing the closing song

We have mentioned processionals in a previous section. If the environment allows, there is a power in emotional transition by walking in line, out of the every day, and into that special time and space, even if it's just for a few feet.

Things to Do with Cremation Remains

The cremation remains (cremains) are ground-up bones with mixed-size pieces, like heavy river sand. They aren't light and fluffy like wood ashes. The crematorium can provide a basic box, usually plastic, for the ashes, or there are fancier boxes and urns that can be purchased or made by loved ones. Some choose to display the box with the ashes on an honored shelf in the home; others want to distribute the ashes in meaningful places; and still others want to bury the container in a special place. In reality, there are probably many cremains containers stored in closets and other places because the family simply can't decide what to do or just aren't emotionally ready to make that decision. Ashes can be spread or kept in one or many locations. Think about how important it is to you or your loved ones to be able to visit the location where the ashes are buried or scattered in the years to come.

Imagine...

An adult son or daughter putting a small decorative and sturdy container of some remains in their golf club bag to help remember the good times and life lessons shared as they played golf together...

Here are a few of the many ways to use the ashes:

- Toss them up into the wind, overlooking a cliff or the sea. (Note: Check first to see which way the wind is blowing so the ashes will go where they are intended, not back in someone's face or onto their clothes.)

- Plant a memorial tree or bush and pour them into the bottom of the planting hole.

- Bury them in a heart-shaped trench and put a marker in the middle.

- Divide and sprinkle them at favorite vacation spots.

- Take them to a destination the deceased had wanted to visit.

- Sprinkle them along a nature trail.

- Sprinkle from a cruise ship late at night, with the wind blowing away from you.

- Bury them next to a favorite pet when the inevitable time comes.

- Mix them into the cement for a stepping-stone for the garden.

- Mix them into the paint for a picture or a sculpture.

- Wear a bit of them in a locket or other jewelry made for this purpose.

- Bury them in a pre-bought plot or in the cremation area of modern cemeteries.

- Put a bit of them into a bag that you fit inside or your bicycle handlebars
- Put some in a decorative item that you hang from the rearview mirror of your car.
- Put a bit of them into a decorative bag that you keep in your luggage, if you travel regularly.
- There are many service providers to help you do unusual things with the cremains. Here are a few of the dozens you'll find on the Internet:
- Include them in ocean reef building structures.
- Include them in ocean bottom art sculptures for divers to enjoy and explore.
- Mix them in a fireworks rocket.
- Compress a bit of them into a manmade diamond.
- Send a bit of them into space.
- Put some of them into an hourglass timer.
- Mix or include them into all kinds of jewelry or sculptures.
- Put a bit of them into any caliber of ammunition you like.
- Mix them into paint to make all kinds of art. Grandma can be on and in the art.

Wherever you are or whatever you do, a ceremony helps to distinguish this as a special time. While your ceremony may be similar to those mentioned previously, here are some specific activities:

- Pass the container to each person so that all will have a last touch and a last word.

- Have each person write a parting message to be included in a separate container for burial at the site. Give each person the opportunity to read the note aloud, if they wish.

- If children are involved, you might ask if they would like to decorate the box for the ashes or the notes.

Graveside Services

These are also known in the funeral trade as direct burial, internment, or committals. Families may opt for a simple graveside or committal service, especially if there will be few people in attendance or if finances are tight.

Many families do not have life insurance, burial insurance, or even cash in their savings account. With funeral and memorial service arrangements sometimes costing thousands of dollars, the surviving family often has to make some tough decisions. Paying for a congregational space, renting a reception hall, paying for food, flowers, programs, and hired-vehicle processional escorts can easily add a substantial cost to the funeral. There is much less expense when the service is short and there is no reception following.

Even if cost is not a factor, some families choose a smaller, more informal setting for their last goodbyes. Graveside services are usually short, twenty to thirty minutes, and are held at the cemetery where the body will be placed in the ground. By their nature, graveside services are usually designed for small groups that will fit under the cemetery's canopy in case of rain.

Traditionally, graveside services are led by a member of the clergy, but certainly can be led by anyone. Trained funeral officiants bring specialized skills, materials, and experience to planning, coordinating, and leading the service, which tends to be more formal. The main purpose is to be with the body where it is being laid to rest.

A shorter graveside service is beneficial to those who are standing through the entire service, and it works well for those who must return to work. On the other hand, some family members may regret that there was no time to talk about or memorialize their loved one. They may be left wanting for more to continue their grieving process. In addition, in a cemetery there is no place to go for commiserating or socializing with someone you haven't seen for a long time. Everyone tends to go their separate way right after the service unless there is an invitation to a home or restaurant.

At traditional cemeteries, ten to twenty chairs are usually provided. The standard arrangement is in straight rows facing outward – less intimacy than the circle or U-shape we discuss in other chapters. Sometimes the initial part of the ceremony is conducted while guests stand in a circle under the canopy. This provides an opportunity for participants to sing, share, or hold hands during this part of the ceremony. In most cases, there won't be any sound system, so ask the officiant to request that participants speak loudly enough for everyone to hear.

Before the casket is lowered, people may stand around it for a last farewell. Ask them to gather in closely and perhaps hold hands around the casket. This human touch can be helpful to the healing and support process.

There are cultural, ethnic, and religious traditions of others that you may want to consider. For some, either symbolically or earnestly covering the buried casket with dirt is meaningful. You may want to ask for or bring several shovels.

As an alternative, provide loose flowers to individually or collectively drop onto the lowered casket. This can be done silently after a reading or while allowing each person who wishes to say something about the loved one. If the burial immediately follows a memorial service that includes many flowers, you may want someone to take apart a couple of arrangements and bring the individual flowers to the graveside service for people to drop into the grave.

The amount of religious content is up to you. As we've said in other parts of this book, there are considerations to be made between what the deceased may have wanted to be said and what the family needs or wants to hear and experience.

The graveside is often a place where a military honor guard ceremony is held. See the section on veterans for more information on this topic. The military part of the ceremony is more formal and somber, so you may not wish to end your memorial service with that mood for your guests. Military honor guards may have specific routines, depending on rank, but they are usually accommodating and willing to participate in any way you prefer. Some even act as pallbearers, escorting the casket from the hearse to the gravesite.

If a military honor guard is not used, we suggest letting various guests have the honor of escorting the casket along the short journey from the hearse to the gravesite. If you have a large number of people you wish to include, you can have different groups take turns for several yards at a time: relatives, then co-workers, then social friends, for example. Or you can have many hands touching the casket as it is rolled or carried along.

Arrange to have the hearse parked further away to make the journey more meaningful. In many cultures and traditions through the ages, the act of the community escorting the body was a major part of the funeral event itself. Walking for the length of time it takes to sing a meaningful song together will add to the emotional impact.

Even though food isn't usually served at a graveside ceremony, you may want to have a beverage to perform a toast to the departed or include something the loved one loved to eat or prepare for others. Some have arranged to have an ice cream or food truck show up at the end of the service to serve refreshments. This adds yet another layer of remembrance and certainly is something that won't be soon forgotten.

Record the ceremony, if possible. Use a family friend, not someone who will be participating in the ceremony, to do the recording. Be aware that wind outdoors will create an annoying sound on a recording, so use a wind baffle on a wireless or shotgun microphone, especially if the camera is more than eight feet from the people who will be speaking or performing. Many professional officiants, funeral homes, or cemeteries have a battery-operated sound system, so ask about using this when appropriate.

Earth-Friendly Burials and Home Funerals

There are new earth-friendly products and services coming on the market every day. For decades there have been objections to the commercialization and cost associated with burials. Over the decades, thousands of tons of concrete, metals of all kinds, lumber, and chemicals have been buried along with our loved ones. Environmentally conscious families have been finding other options. According to the National Funeral Directors Association, the percentage of cremations has increased in virtually every US state.

While cremation requires fewer resources than burial, a growing population is seeking even more environmentally conscious alternatives. Associations and consultants are helping families go back to older traditions. Home funerals and services can include preparing the body at home and having visitations and ceremonies in the home.

The family may bury their loved one in a simple natural fabric or a casket made of natural materials, without attempting to preserve the body in any way. Plain cardboard and fiberboard containers are being personalized with handmade decorations or drawings and handwritten sentiments. Other containers are made of wicker, soft woods, or compressed paper. Local regulations affect how many of these alternatives are offered. The UK and Australia seem to be leading the way.

At the vast majority of burials, the funeral home will have the casket placed on top of a mechanical lowering device. Instead of using the lowering device, you may want to request that the lowering be done by hand, by family and friends who are present. Several articles, written by families who took this approach, indicate this ritual was a very meaningful act of closure. This is the way families have buried their dead for eons.

Imagine…

A wild meadow cemetery area with the grown children of the loved one digging the grave where their father will be buried. And ceremony attendees tossing the soil back over the casket or urn with their thoughts and messages of love…

At some natural burial cemeteries, you are allowed to dig the grave of your loved one. We saw a powerful video story of three strong young men digging the grave of their grandmother in a meadow cemetery. The process took several hours and was very meaningful as they reminisced and cried with sadness and laughter as they dug the grave together. They lowered their grandmother into the hole. She was wrapped in a decorated cloth shroud. As part of their ceremony, the family filled the hole and laid the carefully dug-up grass on top of the grave, just the way the woman had talked about for years. "No muss, no fuss" was her often-heard request. The family made a drawing of the field and surrounding landmarks to remember where she lay. That story will live on in the stories told to their children and grandchildren.

To find out more, use web searches with the following key words:

- Cardboard casket
- Death midwife
- DIY funeral
- Earth-friendly cemeteries
- Earth-friendly burial
- Earth-friendly funerals
- Eco-burial
- Eco-caskets

- Eco-cemeteries

- Green burial

- Green cemeteries

- Home funeral advice

- Home funeral

- Home funeral service

- Natural burial

- Natural material caskets

- Pasture cemetery

- Woodland burial

- Woodland cemetery

Here are some websites to get you started:

- **NatureDeath.org.uk** has a long list of resources and links, especially for those in the United Kingdom; however, the advice given is universal.

- **Crossings.net** is a home funeral and green burial resource center "to foster the integration of dying and after-death care back into our family and community life."

- **SacredCrossings.com** offers ministerial services, education, and guidance for green, cost-effective funerals at home and death midwife training.

- **MemorialEcosystems.com** provides advice and resources on woodland burials.

- **HoneyCreekWoodlands.com** is a natural burial cemetery near Atlanta, GA.

- **FinalPassages.org** is dedicated to a compassionate and dignified alternative to current funeral practices.

- **HomeFuneralAlliance.org** is a group of home funeral service providers and advocates.

- **UndertakenWithLove.org** offers a free home funeral guide for congregations and communities.

- **DonnaBelk.com** includes a blog and many resources. Donna is a death midwife and one of the authors of the *Undertaken with Love* manual and the HomeFuneralDirectory.com website.

- **HomeFuneralDirectory.com** is a resource-filled website hosted by Donna Belk and Sandy Booth. It includes a list of links to related videos.

Mortuaries and funeral homes can also be of service with green burials and home funerals. Funeral homes can provide an indoor space for a memorial service followed by a more intimate graveside service at a green burial site.

While funeral homes benefit by selling caskets, by law, American funeral homes must accept and use caskets that the family may buy from other suppliers. In today's evolving market, most are being more flexible and creative with family requests. They will even make arrangements to hold the memorial services at alternative locations if the traditional environment of most mortuaries doesn't fit your personality.

US Military and Veteran Ceremonies

In the US, as in other countries, veterans of World War II and their spouses are rapidly passing. Large national veteran cemeteries conduct ten or more funerals a day. Because of this, military honor guards have had to limit the amount of time allocated for each service. Call the US Department of Veterans Affairs at (800) 535-1117 to learn more.

Each military branch may provide different kinds of services, and those options may vary according to location. Ask about variables provided for active duty members, retirees, and veterans serving fewer than 20 years, as well as Medal of Honor recipients. There are differing services available for each.

All of the ceremonies at a military cemetery are done at designated areas, not at the gravesite. An honor guard may be able to escort the casket to the burial site. Check with your cemetery coordinator. The size of the area, and thus the number people who can attend, also varies. Space for between 40 and 75 people is the average. Some ceremony areas have seating only for the family and others stand behind them. Check seating availability in advance.

You are allowed one honor guard service whether it is held at a national veteran cemetery or another venue. Local funeral service providers usually make the arrangements with the military and will guide you in the process. Although there are standard procedures for the honor guard, you can make special requests. In larger communities, there are usually enough veteran volunteers from each of the branches of service to have their own honor guard; in others, a mixed-branch honor guard is available.

To qualify for national cemetery benefits, contact the national call center as soon as possible, even before the death, to get the proper paperwork submitted and processed in time. The location of a burial site within a national cemetery cannot be reserved. The exception is that graves are dug double-deep so a spouse or the veteran, whoever dies second, will go into the same grave. Families can choose any national military cemetery for burial of the casket or storage of the cremation remains; they just have to arrange for transport of the body or cremains. Families can purchase additional flags online to be folded and presented to family members by the honor guard.

Ceremony areas are only available for between 20 to 30 minutes, so larger and longer memorial services will need to be conducted at other locations. The family and others then go to the cemetery for the interment or burial ceremony. In the US, it is traditional for the bugle player to play "Taps" at the end of the day or at the end of the memorial service. Similarly, "Reveille" is played at the beginning of a new day. If you choose to have "Reveille" played, tell your guests why this is significant for your loved one. Funerals go on regardless of the weather. In frozen areas, hundreds of gravesites are dug in advance and covered with wood. At the time of the burial, the grave is filled with leaves or other mulch until it can be filled with soil.

Here are some logistical considerations:

- You might decide to leave one chair vacant to include the deceased veteran's uniform or boots.

- Ask about a sound system, and be prepared to bring your own.

- You supply your own officiant to create and lead the service.

The VA (Veterans Administration) has additional information on their website at VA.gov.

In one service that we attended, the honor guard started the service by playing "Taps" from the back of the room, then brought the folded flag into the sanctuary, placed it on a table in front of the guests, and left the room. To close the service, the honor guard returned to unfold, display, and refold the flag in a very ceremonial manner before presenting it to one of the daughters. In this situation, a celebratory service of a much-loved and admired man ended in a somber and reverent tone. The family and guests left the sanctuary in almost complete silence. Think about how you want your service to end when planning a military component.

For veterans of other countries, these statements should provide you with a starting point for questions to ask when you contact your country's military burial offices. If the above description of a military funeral sounds too formal, you might opt for a smaller memorial service that suits the style and demeanor of the soldier who has died. This could better suit the family's budget, transportation needs, and emotional well-being.

PART II

Additional Ways to Bring Together Family and Friends

CHAPTER 18
Conversations and Activities During the Last Days

The dying process can begin long before the actual death occurs, and the grieving can go on long after. Pulitzer Prize winner Ellen Goodman has written *The Conversation Project* about the importance of having a real conversation about end-of-life wishes for yourself and others. Goodman says that the conversation is a gift that caregivers, parents, and children can give to each other.

In her book, Goodman reports that more than half of all Americans have not communicated anything about their death to those they love. This oversight places a heavy burden of decision-making on those left behind after a loved one dies. Some of the most important conversations can take place well before the end is near. Since we never know how or when the end will come, it is best to talk about the dying process and death itself well in advance, even when we are healthy. After all, most of us don't plan to die at a particular time, so the sooner we talk about it the better.

Such conversations can be tricky. What to say? When and how to bring up the subject of death and dying? What should be talked about? No matter when you have the conversation, it will help your family make important decisions.

If possible, record the conversation and take notes to avoid confusion or misunderstandings with family caregivers and decision-makers. We have included ideas and activities that can be useful to you and your family in the lists below.

Questions to Stimulate Important Conversations

- Who do you want with you in your last days and hours?

- Which of your family and "friends" do you not want to be with you in your last days and hours?

- Are there things that you would like to say to particular people before you die? (love, forgiveness, regrets, etc.)

- Are there things left for you to do before you say, "I'm ready to die"?

- What guidelines should we have for medicating you for pain relief? What level of pain are you willing to endure in order to stay alert? If you are unable to talk, what signal can we use so we know when you have endured enough and want additional or no additional medication?

- Is there an occasion or situation that you want to be a part of before you let go of your life? Hospitals and hospices often report that people will rally to see someone in particular or to find out who was elected president.

- Are there religious or spiritual rites or rituals you want performed with or for you? Who would you like to do them?

- What extra measures should be used to keep you alive if you are awake, aware, or in a coma?

- What are financial considerations related to your care? Do you approve that your care providers can spend every cent you have or put family into long-term debt to keep you alive a little longer? Are you concerned that the money spent during your last days would be better spent going to the grandchildren's college funds?

- Where are the papers that give the care providers instructions on whether to extend your life or let you go (for instance, DNR - Do Not Resuscitate, Durable Power of Attorney)?

For more information on Ellen Goodman's topics, go to TheConversationProject.org.

Activities that Can Make a Difference
During the Last Stages of Life

While it may feel uncomfortable to be planning for the inevitable, if you plan you will be able to better anticipate what you can do during this critical time. Take advantage of the months, days, or hours you have left so both the family and the dying loved one can benefit. Some ideas:

- Assign someone to be the gatekeeper. Schedule the number and combinations of visitors. Are there people that the dying person would rather not see or speak with? This is not a place or time for annoying or angry people.

- If your loved one is in a small or shared room in a hospital or care facility, ask about the availability of a larger, more private space when several people will be coming to say their goodbyes.

- "Sing out" songs are meaningful and memorable if the loved one approves and people are available.

Imagine...

Family and friends are gathered around your loved one, singing their favorite songs. A song leader keeps everyone singing in tempo...

This will be therapeutic, meaningful, and memorable for everyone involved. You could also use familiar recorded music.

See the music section for soothing songs to hum, sing, or play. A 2014 Sundance Film Festival documentary winner demonstrates the power of a person's nostalgic music to help their spirit reawaken like nothing else can. See the film and watch interviews with the producer on the web: "Alive Inside: A Story of Music and Memory" by Michael Rossato-Bennett.

Learn about what to expect and observe in the next and last stages, as death approaches. There are many good books, articles, and videos for you to read, watch, and share. They will greatly reduce the stress and anxiety for those who have gathered to share this time and provide support. Our website contains videos and book titles of at least two experts, Dr. Lani Leary and Barbara Karnes, RN.

Good Things to Say in the Last Hours

The last hours of life can be emotional and stressful for all involved. Sometimes it is difficult to come up with something truthful and meaningful to say. Here are some suggestions:

- We are with you.
- We love you.
- We will always remember you.
- We will be okay.
- We give you our blessings to go and release your ties with us.

- I understand that you have to go.

Professionals say that the last thing to go is often a person's hearing, so be mindful of what you say and how you say it. Even if your loved one can no longer hear or speak, gentle touch is often the best expression of all.

A Time for the Family to Connect

Gathering as the loved one is dying may bring together family from far and near. Family members may not have seen each other in a long time, so plan for a family get-together before friends and community members get involved. This is a part of the support and healing process. If there are hard feelings between family members, specify that at least at this one gathering, only fond memories are to be shared.

Creating a Nurturing Environment
as the End Draws Near

- Reduce the brightness of the room lighting to create a relaxed atmosphere. (Have a dimmer installed or have an optional lamp with a 40 or 60 watt equivalent bulb.) One candle in a small room is often enough. Be aware that some people will be sensitive to candle smoke and aroma, especially if they are lit for many hours.

- Think about the nostalgia of particular smells to bring back fond memories, such as freshly baked cookies or nostalgic ethnic foods, or perhaps the perfume or aftershave lotion of a deceased spouse.

- Use a family heirloom quilt as a blanket for your loved one.

- Change the pictures on the wall by including framed pictures of relatives who have come to visit, or use a bulletin board or easel to display pictures.

- Be aware of the sounds and conversations in the room or within earshot of your loved one. Situations often change day to day and hour to hour, or the person may appear to be sleeping. Don't assume that the person can't hear what you are saying.

- Be aware of ambient sounds. Sometimes background chatter can be comforting; other times it can be irritating or upsetting.

- Many times, the elderly and those with hearing loss will take out or not have their hearing aids when they are in their last days and hours, especially in the hospital. They may not hear what people have to say, or the sound may be distorted. You may need a person to sit near her, looking directly at her and speaking clearly and more slowly than normal, to interpret. Even when hearing aids are in place, it is difficult to understand multiple conversations.

- Memory can be affected near the end of life. Announce each visitor's name and their connection with the person if they are not immediately recognized. Oftentimes, relatives and friends who come to visit haven't been seen in many years. People look different, especially growing children. Depending on the situation, it may be valuable to do the introduction every time you speak to your loved one.

- Make it easier and more meaningful for kids to participate. In the past, children were "sheltered" from the situation and told to go out and play. We now know that children internalize many misconceptions when this happens, often blaming themselves for what is going on. Explain in advance, in age-appropriate ways, what the children will see, hear, and experience when they are with the dying person and grieving relatives. Go to our website for books and articles on what, when, and how to share about the dying experience with children.

- It may be valuable to guide visitors on what to say and how to act around the dying person. A person's religious or nonreligious beliefs, as well as cultural traditions, often color what people want to say or hear. Perhaps someone in your family cannot face the facts or they are eternal optimists, saying things like "Mom, you're looking good" or "As soon as you can start eating solid food, you're going to get better." Is this going to help or hinder the situation?

A loved one might help prepare others for the conversation or last words ahead. Here are some examples:

- He knows he is dying and doesn't want to see pity or sadness on your face.

- He wants to carry on a normal conversation about life and what is going on with you, even though he knows he is dying.

- He wants to tell you about some things.

- He can't talk, but he can hear. Tell him how much he has meant to you.

- He knows he only has a short time left. Don't waste it by pretending, saying, "I'll check in with you next week."

- He may say things that don't make sense, such as mentioning he has spoken with his deceased wife. Just go along with it and inquire about the details as if it were true.

Imagine…

A woman in her senior years is cuddled closely to her fading mother, sharing together those tender words and thoughts they rarely if ever were willing or able to say before…

Here are the kinds of things you can say that could make a world of difference:

- Bob, I've cherished our friendship and great conversations. I'm really going to miss you.
- Dad, you've been a wonderful role model in so many ways – in your living and in your dying.
- Because of your teaching, I'm going to be OK, even though I'm going to miss you more than I can even imagine.
- Mom, it seems so strange to say this, but I want you to know that any time you want to let go, do it. If you are ready, we will be ready and OK.

In advance, discuss with your loved one if there are any items to be passed down or distributed. Is the dying person fit enough to make the presentation of desired objects? Especially at a time like this, the old adage is true: "One man's trash is another man's treasure." Sometimes a very plain and utilitarian object will be desired and treasured, such as the birthday cake pan that Grandma used to make cakes for you. Dave still uses his grandmother's salt shaker, and Beverly uses her great-grandmother's turkey platter.

Resources for End-of-Life Experiences

Here are a few resources to consider:

- No One Has to Die Alone - *Preparing for a Meaningful Death* by Lani Leary, PhD. She has been with more than 500 people during their last hours and has appeared on Ted.com. Go to DrLaniLeary.com.

- *It's OK to Die* by Dr. Monica Williams-Murphy, MD. Preparation prevents suffering and creates opportunities for peace, closure, and even healing. Go to OkToDie.com.

- *Daddy This Is It - Being with my Dying Dad* by Julie Saeger Nierenberg. The exchanges of words and emotion between the author's father and the extended family provide a model for what is possible in end-of-life communication and closure.

- The Esse Institute, founded by Virginia Seno, PhD, teaches how to talk about death and dying, meeting the needs of patients, families, and the bereaved. Go to EsseInstitute.com.

- EngageWithGrace.org, founded by Alexandra Drane and Matthew Holt, provides a powerful personal story video on five questions to ask your loved ones about what they want you to do at their end of life.

- *The Final Act of Living: Reflections of a Long-time Hospice Nurse* by Barbara Karnes, who has dedicated the last thirty-two years of her life to the education, care, and comforting of dying people and their loved ones. The most useful things she's learned along the way have been distilled into her several books, booklets, and DVDs found at BKBooks.com.

CHAPTER 19

Recording Family Personalities and Stories as a Legacy

When families are gathered, fond memories are usually shared; yet, so often, those stories are relegated to memory only. A picture is worth a thousand words, and a video is worth a thousand pictures. If you are considering recording, don't put it off. Recording family personalities and stories provides a priceless legacy and there may not be another opportunity due to mental or physical decline or even death.

Weddings, graduations, memorial services, and other lifecycle events are in essence family reunions around a special occasion. Take advantage of planned and unplanned gatherings to set aside intentional time to share and record the fond memories of and about your loved ones. This is a priceless gift to your immediate and extended family to pass on the history, personal anecdotes, and personality of family members at this point in time.

StoryCorps segments on National Public Radio provide the opportunity to record, share, and preserve the stories of our lives. Go to StoryCorps.org for examples of the poignant stories shared. Create your own family archive of stories to document who you are, where you came from, and how you came to be the family you are today.

For other examples of what to share go to ThisIBelieve.org. More than 100,000 everyday Americans have shared their core values in recorded and written essays since acclaimed journalist Edward R. Murrow started this in 1951.

Recordings can:

- Celebrate and honor the sheer joy of storytelling.
- Honor the past and pay tribute to people who have shaped your life.
- Created a priceless legacy of memories and stories for generations.
- Explain your actions and decisions, providing insight and perspective.
- Communicate your values, beliefs, and ethics.
- Offer advice to your children (or anyone else!) based on your mistakes, successes, and observations.
- Set the record straight and help you and others achieve peace of mind.

Imagine...

An elder is sharing the background stories of his favorite possessions, which are laid out on a table in front of him. He also shares with the grandchildren how to fold paper hats and other fun things that they can do for others and remember him in the process...

- Tell the stories about the special things you own. This idea is similar to telling about items with provenance (history of the item) featured on "Antiques Roadshow," a popular TV show on public broadcasting. The tarnished candlesticks in the attic may be yard sale material, but if we knew that Winston Churchill gave it to Great Aunt Bessie, it becomes a priceless family heirloom. Make sure your children and grandchildren know and appreciate the stories associated with your treasured items and collectibles, so these heirlooms items are not inadvertently discarded.

Although having a professional videographer helps, you don't have to go that route. Whatever memories you capture will be appreciated by those who follow. If you've never thought of doing this before, we share some ideas to get things rolling in the list below.

Ways to Share Your Stories, Heritage, Legacy and Talents

- Grandpa reads the favorite stories of his own kids while they were growing up so that the future children will hear the stories read by him.
- Grandma explains the meaning of special words and phrases from her heritage to strengthen the ethnic identity of the grandchildren.

- Grandpa does a "show and tell" of items in his toolbox that the grandchildren will inherit one day.

- Mom displays the Ellis Island documents and heirlooms she inherited.

- A family talent show is fun and showcases traditional strange talents. The Johnson family sings, niece Emily plays the violin, cousin Mike shows off magic tricks, brother Sid shows how he makes paper hats, and you do the tap dance you learned as a child.

- Everyone joins in to fill in the missing parts of a large family tree. People bring documents and pictures for "show and tell" about the items.

- Individuals or groups share the backstories of old family photos.

- If you will be downsizing, do a "show and tell" about memorabilia that you need to let go of as you prepare to move to a smaller place. Give a walking tour of your home and share the experiences and fond memories of each area of the house and yard.

- Be interviewed by a loved one to create an in-depth video memoir.

- Share "An Ethical Will" that offers a personal sharing of your values, wisdom, regrets, lessons learned, and confessions that you hope will heal relationship pain, provide insights into your actions, and share wisdom that you hope will be an inspiration and guide for the next generation. This is a meaningful and powerful inheritance that only you can give. The Ethical Will video is a sharing of the ideas and concepts that you hold as valued and important. There are many articles, online videos, and books with ideas and materials for writing or recording your ethical will. Ethical Wills can be recorded by people of any age; it is amazing what you will hear from children and young people.

- Cook together to share stories, heritage recipes, and the personalities that make your family unique and memorable. For inspiration, see past episodes of the American Cooking Channel show "My Grandmother's Ravioli," hosted by Mo Rocca. He travels the country and makes treasured recipes with a wide variety of grandparents. Go to CookingChannelTV.com to find the show.

Prepare the Participants

- Provide a list of questions ahead of time to help participants prepare for the interview. This can jog their memories about events or people the person had nearly forgotten.

- Have participants make notes of names, dates, and places to better recall them during recorded conversations.

- Using websites like Ancestry.com, conduct advance research on your family genealogy to help stimulate the conversation.

- Discuss what is most interesting and worth preserving. It's easy to get sidetracked with unexpected "just-thought-of-it" remembrances. You may decide to just go with the natural flow of the conversation or redirect participants to get back on track with the original train of thought.

Maintain the Flow of Conversation

- Have a glass of water nearby. Storytelling will whip up the adrenaline and dry out the mouth.

- Have an extra person on hand to answer the phone or the doorbell, let the dog in or out, and generally assist in keeping the recording area quiet.

- If someone says they cannot remember anything, ask questions to help prompt memories.

- Small mementos add interest to your family history. For instance, record what is inside a person's wallet, purse, or a junk drawer and notice items in display cabinets.

- Take notes to keep track of follow-up questions.

Prompt Lively and Informative Conversations

- Ask open-ended questions that go beyond the facts and yes-or-no answers. See HeartfeltMemorialServices.com for questions and topics.

- Avoid asking questions that include "the best," "the most," or "our favorite." Most people freeze up trying to think of and prioritize all of their options.

- Plan conversations and recordings around a loved one's schedule and the time of day. Will he be taking medication that will make him drowsy?

- If you are interviewing a frail or elderly individual, start with questions about their memories or knowledge of their parents, grandparents, and siblings. Make sure their energy is up as they are recalling this priceless information.

- When asking about other people, establish the basic information such as dates and places and where they were born, died, or grew up. Capture addresses if possible.

- Gather folklore and stories passed down from one generation to the next: "My father said he was…"

- Bring out the high school yearbook to share the messages friends wrote and let the memories flood back.

Below are some questions to ask one participant or everyone in a group. There are many more at HeartfeltMemorialServices.com and MemoryKeepersVideo.com. In addition, StoryCorps.org has lists of questions and recordings from their segments on National Public Radio to inspire you.

Sample Questions for Kids to Ask Elders

- What advice do you have that you always want me to remember?

- What is the story about your given name? Do you like your name or is there another one you would prefer?

- When and where were you born?

- Describe what your home looked like: your bedroom, your yard, etc.

- How did you get to school?

- Were you in the "in" crowd or the "out" crowd when you were a teenager? What was it like?

- What foods didn't you like as a kid?

- Who was a favorite teacher and why?

- What were some favorite playground games? Will you teach me?

- Tell me about some family trips.

- What were your parents like?

- Did you get an allowance? How much? What could you buy with it?

- What did you do to earn money as a kid?

- What were the rules about dating?

- What dances did you do as a teenager? (Show me!)

- Do you know how to swim? How did you learn?

- Tell me about some of your good friend adventures and memorable experiences.

- When and how did you learned to drive a car?

- Do you wish you treated your brother(s) or sister(s) differently?

- What advice do you have for helping to create a really happy family?

- What were your hopes and dreams while you were growing up?

- What were your holiday traditions?

- What are some tasty food items you like to make?

Parenthood

- How did you find out that you were going to be a parent for the first time?

- How many children did you have? What were their names, birthdates, and birthplaces?

- Do you remember anything that your children did when they were small that really amazed you?

- What was a funny thing you can remember that one of your children said or did?

- If you had it to do all over again, in what ways would you change the way you raised your family?

Your Work and Career

- As a child, what did you want to be when you grew up?

- What was your first job? What kinds of jobs have you had?

- How did you decide on your career?

- What did you think about the money you were earning?

- How long did you have to work each day at your jobs?

Religious, Political, Social, and Economic Preferences

- What is your current religious identity and why?

- Why do you belong to the congregation that you attend?

- How do you live differently because of your religious beliefs or participation?

- Were there any special religious events in your life?

- Did you have a favorite verse, hymn, song, or religious ritual?

- Tell me about your religious or spiritual beliefs in as much detail as you can.

Philosophical Questions

- As your life's journey unfolded, how has your behavior towards others changed?

- How did your description of yourself change through the years? ("In my youth I would say that I was…," "In my middle years I was…," and "Now, I am…") How did those self-descriptions affect or guide you throughout your life?

- What were some hard choices you had to make? How did they work out?

- Did someone change the course of your life? Why and how?

- What has been on your bucket list? Which one can we help you accomplish soon'?

- What are common characteristics of your close friends?

- What would you still like to learn or do better?

How to Record Your Memories

Sound

Use handheld or lapel microphones, whenever possible, to reduce surrounding noise. Microphones built into video cameras often pick up a large empty room echo that you cannot hear with your ears but can hear on the playback. When recording, shut off as many mechanical devices as possible, such as dishwashers and air conditioners, and ask neighbors to hold off using their lawnmower or weed whacker or put their barking dog inside.

Lighting

Video loves lights. If possible, use two or three 100 watt, spiral "daylight" bulbs for an average living room space. Make sure the lights aren't shining in the eyes of the people on camera. Use lights even if there is plenty of sunlight coming in. Often, clouds go by or the sun begins to set. Conversations can continue for one to two hours, and good lighting is important.

Background

Have your filming area be as uncluttered as possible. Avoid pointing the camera at lights and lamps in the background. They adversely affect how the camera lights up your subjects.

Seating

Include everyone talking in a single, wide-angle shot. Zoom in for close-ups. When recording just two or three people, have them sit close to each other in a V-shape, so it is easier for them to look at each other or the camera. For a larger group, arrange everyone in a U-shape. Decide whether the participants should have a conversation among each other or if each participant needs to look in the camera to talk.

Props

If you plan to show photos or memorabilia, position the seating to one side of the "set" so that the memorabilia and the people can be seen at the same time. To focus on pictures or nostalgic items, you might want to sit around a table. If you are going to sit on a sofa or in an easy chair, have a TV tray or other side table(s) within arm's reach. Organize the pictures and objects in advance to help tell the stories in a sequence.

Sequence

Determine the focus of the video and how long you will record. Will you have just one session or several? Plan for one to two hours per session. Beyond that, most people become tired and need a break. Make sure the story has a beginning, middle, and end. Have someone introduce the purpose of the gathering, participants, date, and place. End your video with summarizing and closing words.

Editing the Recording

Don't go overboard with special effects when you edit the video. They can distract from the story. Use pictures of referenced people, places, and things as they complement the stories told.

Sharing the Video with Your Family

As of this writing, saving your videos in an MP4 format can help reduce file size and make the videos more appropriate for sharing. WeTransfer.com is a free service used to share video up to two gigabytes. Technology changes quickly. Refer to our website and YouTube for the most updated way to store and share long videos.

CHAPTER 20

Plan a Meaningful Celebration of Life Party

Dave's 80-something mom has admonished the family for years by saying, "I don't care what you do about me when I die. Come and see me now, while I am able to enjoy the visit. Tell me what you want to say to my face. I won't hear you when I'm gone." While Dave's mom is talking about a visit, let's take the thought a step further.

While Your Friend is Still Here to Enjoy It

A friend who had been told he didn't have much longer to live said, "I don't want a funeral, I want a party!" What would that party look like if we knew that our friend would soon be gone? Think in terms of the old TV shows "This is Your Life" or the Friars Club roasts where celebrities made fun of and saluted each other. (You can see some of these shows on YouTube.) It's time for a Celebration-of-Life party!

Friends of Chris Daley did just that. Diagnosed with a terminal illness and opting not to go through more treatment that would only delay the inevitable, Chris agreed to let her husband and friends put on a party of a lifetime… just for her. The place was packed. It was a potluck dinner, with friends coming early and staying late. There was a slide show, a table of photos, remembrances of friends from every phase of her life, music, dance, and a speech of appreciation from Chris to her family and friends. Many attended the local Center for Spiritual Living, so there were plenty of like-minded souls on hand to celebrate her life, not just grieve for her upcoming death.

The celebration-of-life event you plan doesn't have to be just a party with laughter and dancing; it can be a gathering to suit your friend's personality and state of mind. One common characteristic of the most successful celebration-of-life parties is that sometime during the event, perhaps after everyone has arrived, the group is called together for a more thoughtful and emotional transition. The leader could begin with the lighting of a candle and a reminder of why the group has gotten together and officially recognize the guest of honor. This is a good opportunity to welcome friends and family who have come to contribute to the occasion. A few people may want to say words of love, admiration, and appreciation, some of which may not be appropriate at a traditional funeral service. Letters from dear friends and family, who could not attend, can also be read. If appropriate, adding a fun or sentimental song, sung by all of the guests holding hands in a circle around the guest of honor, would be an emotional and memorable ceremony. If it is an expressive group, they could pass around a flower or other symbolic object, each sharing a few thoughtful words. Look for some of the other activities mentioned in Part I of this book. The fact that you gathered together for a short time often brings the sense of honor and sentimentality that will make the celebration-of-life party even more meaningful.

If any of your family members would consider it macabre to plan a service around someone's eventual death, consider having friends and family put together a similar kind of celebration-of-life party for an upcoming birthday or anniversary. Doesn't that make sense? If a friend would spend the money to attend your funeral or memorial service across the country, wouldn't her money and time be better spent visiting with a loved one while they are still around to visit? Planning ahead for a gathering is much less expensive than showing up just after the death.

Beverly and her childhood girlfriend, Marie, had a similar experience. Their close and wonderful high school friend, Linda Nevitte, had been diagnosed with a fatal disease. She was still feeling quite well, and a friend gifted her with a timeshare week at a resort near where she lived in Virginia. Marie and Beverly flew up from Florida and Georgia to meet her and take her to the resort. They all ate heartily, drank wine, hiked, visited shops and restaurants, and had a poignant, fun time.

As the end came near for Linda, we knew she was being taken care of by family and friends in Virginia. Marie and Beverly didn't need to be there for her death. They had been important parts of her life, and that is what mattered most to Linda. So to start planning a loved one's celebration-of-life gathering, ask: What are their favorite songs or readings? Who will be the master of ceremonies? Are there particular photos you would like to use? Who will speak or give remembrances?

A celebration-of-life party does not take the place of a funeral or memorial service that honors and acknowledges your loved one's passing. We have included details about those kinds of ceremonies in other parts of the book.

For a Friend after She Has Gone

Of course, it is not always possible to plan a celebration-of-life party before someone dies, but don't let that stop you from honoring your friend after the fact. The celebration-of-life party can be a time to relax and honor your friend in a unique and unusual way. A good friend, Marcia Briscoe, was remembered in two ways. Her family held a more traditional religious service at a funeral home, and a week later her flamboyant friends got together and threw a more jubilant, laughter-filled party we know she would have loved to attend. Aren't these the kinds of comments you would like to have made after your party?

Barbara, a dear friend of Marcia wrote: "I awoke into this new day with a heart overflowing with joyful appreciation for my community and what love looks like, feels like, and tastes like!

Thank you so much to everyone who showed up last night to honor beautiful Marcia. The evening was filled with magical connection, tender words, and endearing friendship. It took a village to create this tribute in Grand Fashion, not to mention the population of helpers to run vacuum cleaners to sweep up all the boa feathers left on the floor. Each feather is symbolic of the glitter that Marcia brought into our lives. I do believe we have now set a precedent for our congregation of how life can truly be if you reach out and hold the hand of the person to the left and to the right. A special thanks to all who put their hearts and souls into ensuring this event would have Marcia jumping up and down in a full-tilt boogie mode. Indeed, love is all you need, gang. BRING IT ON!!!"

Lexa, a close friend of Marcia wrote: "It was magical. Last night was not only a tribute to Marcia, but a new standard in the power of synergy and the creativity and self-expression possible in community. My heart expanded to a dimension I had never experienced. There was no room for anything but love in that room. And how fitting that was what showed up to honor our dear friend. I'm proud of what we did and eternally altered by the gifts she brought to our lives and continues to bring by her example and the introductions she provided to us to so many of the people in that building last night. Her legacy."

What kind of party would you like to have and for whom? Don't put it off. Do it now.

CHAPTER 21

Remembering You
Many Times and in Many Ways

Times of remembrance come to us many times throughout the year, no matter how long it's been since your loved one has been gone. Time has no relevance. Consider the seventieth anniversary reunion of the Allied Forces on the Banks of Normandy in 2014. Many gathered with their families to share stories, laugh, mourn, and still cry for friends who died and those who are still missing. Have your own moments of remembrance any time you wish.

Take advantage of the following opportunities:

- Holidays
- Anniversaries
- Birthdays
- Locations you are thinking about visiting
- Music around you
- Foods you are smelling or tasting

You are likely to hear comments like this:

- Jimmy would have loved this.

- Grandpa loved this home place.

- Mom's birthday is this week.

- It's our first Christmas without Dad.

- This kitchen smells like Grandma.

- Ginny always loved red roses.

- This is my first birthday without her.

- It's Memorial Day and I'll never forget my buddies who never came home.

We can take these times to remember our loved ones in a more meaningful way. Days or decades are the same when it comes to missing your child or your mom.

Create a Remembrance Ceremony

You can create a remembrance ceremony as a special event or when people are gathered for another purpose, such as a reunion or family wedding. You reflect on and remember one loved one or invoke the names of the many relatives and ancestors who helped to bring your family to that special time and place. Record the event whenever possible. It will be treasured later as the years pass.

Here are some things to consider as you plan your ceremony:

- Lead with words of welcome and introduction.

- Recall memories of your loved one through the different phases of his life.

- Evoke as many of the senses as you can. Consider the suggestions below.

Sight

- Decorate the space.

- Wear something special, perhaps something of his.

- Show family pictures, films, or videos significant to your loved one.

- Watch a favorite movie or TV program that he enjoyed.

Sound

- Play or sing a special song he enjoyed.

- Play a voice recording of your loved one to keep the sound of his voice alive.

Taste

- Eat something he enjoyed or prepared.

- Visit a restaurant that you enjoyed together.

Touch

- Hold, caress, or pass around something that reminds you of him, such as a piece of clothing he wore or something that he also touched.

Smell

- Breathe in nostalgic cologne you identify with him.
- Breathe in the unique smells that surrounded him in his home or workshop.

When we attended a Death Cafe event (DeathCafe.com), a woman shared that she bought dozens of her deceased son's favorite candy bars and gave them away to friends and strangers on the anniversary of his birthday. Friends may not have wanted to bring up the subject of his passing for fear of causing emotional pain, especially since he died a tragic death, but the fact that she was sharing gave them permission to talk about him and show that they cared.

You could even decide to print your loved one's name or a special message on a give-away item to encourage openness and conversation about your loved one. Search the advertising of specialty or promotional products on the Internet to find an appropriate item that would suit your needs.

Appendix I
What Not to Say and What to Say

Relationships can be forever ruined when friends, family, or acquaintances make insensitive remarks to people who are going through terrible times. We suggest to say nothing, rather than spout something that can never be taken back. For instance, when someone:

- has been diagnosed with a terminal illness or long-term
- has just found out about a loved one's diagnosis
- has experienced a sudden loss through a suicide, an accident, or an unexpected death
- is anticipating the loss of a loved one
- is dying and is in hospice care
- is grieving over a loss

We suggest you not give advice, philosophize, preach, admonish, pretend everything will be all right, or show pity. With so many things *not* to say, no wonder many feel at a loss when coming up with the right thing to say. But you can do it. This is an important responsibility of friends and family members, and you are up to the task. While there are many more examples, we decided to use two scenarios: a loved one who is dying and a person who has experienced a loss. In his book, *The Four Things That Matter Most*, Dr. Ira Byock, professor of palliative medicine at Dartmouth-Hitchcock Medical Center in New Hampshire, writes that dying people typically want to hear (and to say) four things: "Please forgive me," "I forgive you," "Thank you," and "I love you."

What Not to Say to Someone Who is Dying

When someone is coming to the end of life, there is a tendency to want to put a Band-Aid on the situation to make it (you) feel better. We suggest that sugarcoating is a waste of precious time. Below are some statements where people are pretending that the end isn't near. (*In parenthesis is what the person dying might be thinking.*)

- We'll be back for a visit next week when Joey gets back from summer camp. (*I won't be alive then.*)
- Now, you know that chocolate cupcake isn't good for you. (*I want to enjoy what I want while I still can.*)
- Now finish up that soup – you have to get more vitamins. (*I don't like this soup and I resent your trying to make me eat it.*)
- There's a football game on… we can watch it together. (*I would rather visit than waste precious time with TV.*)

- I'm bringing your grandkids over for a visit. (*They are way too loud and I am way too tired – please don't.*)

- Shouldn't you be doing physical therapy? (*My muscles don't need to get stronger to die.*)

What to Say to Someone Who is Dying

When we are in the presence of someone who is dying, how can we make this time as meaningful as possible?

Hearing is the last sense to leave the dying person, so even if she becomes unresponsive, many times she can hear you. Be sensitive about what you, care providers, friends, and family are saying and doing. If appropriate, hold her hand or stroke her arm gently as you speak, or even stretch out on the bed with her.

This may be the last time you have a chance to talk to your loved one before the death. Think of how meaningful your last sharing time could be with words like this:

- I'd like to say thank you. You know that you are my favorite aunt, and I'll miss you and remember you always.

- Thank you for being in my life and allowing me to be in yours.

- I knew I could count on you… for your good advice… to make me laugh… to teach me something new…

- You never cease to amaze me… with all the friends you have… your sculptures… the way you can repair anything…

- You've always been a wonderful and inspiring role model for me, like when I couldn't decide what my college major would be.

- I have passed on your guidance to other people, like when you said to let little annoyances roll off your back… when you advised me to wait at least twenty-four hours before responding to an emotional issue…

- Thank you for… your collection of crazy hats… your recipes… the golf lessons because…

- I've always appreciated and admired you for… the way you treated strangers… the way you stood by my brother when he got in trouble…

- You've had a lasting impact on our family by building the cabin in Michigan… recording our family stories… introducing us to the world of gardening…

- Some of my fondest memories of our times together are… learning to scuba dive… touring the Grand Canyon… the river boat ride down the Mississippi River…

These last heartfelt words can be a soothing balm for the giver and the receiver.

What Not to Say to Those Who Are Grieving

It is nearly impossible to gauge where a person is in the grieving process. While being at a loss about what to say to a person grieving is understandable, saying the wrong thing is not appropriate any time. Sometimes, when we are at a loss regarding what to say, we say anything that comes to mind. We end up doing what we would most like to avoid: hurting the person we want to console. Below are some things people might unwittingly say. (*In parenthesis is what the bereaved might be thinking.*)

- **I know exactly how you feel.** (*No, you don't.*) Our reactions to grief are very different. Even if you, too, lost your mother recently, don't assume that your experience was the same as the bereaved.

- **He's in a better place now.** (*How dare you... I want him here with me.*) Even if the one left behind believes in heaven, that statement is difficult to accept. Whether a parent has lost a child, a spouse has lost a mate, or a parent is gone after a long bout with a painful disease, the one left behind doesn't want to talk about that "better place." They would tend to be thinking the better place is with them — *alive.*

- **Don't cry, you'll upset your mother…** or **Your children don't want to see you upset…** or **You need to be strong.** (*I can't hold the tears in for one more minute.*) Expressing your opinion about how someone is responding to or handling a difficult situation is condescending and judgmental. People experience several stages of grief and each person will react differently during the various phases. Just because you believe someone should follow your grieving timetable doesn't mean you are right. It's their grief; let them experience it in whatever way suits them.

- **She looks so natural.** (*Thank you?? The embalmer did a wonderful job.*) If this is an open casket, it is usually best to stay away from comments and judgments unless a loved one wants to talk about it.

- **Let me know if I can help.** (*I can't even think straight. How am I going to remember to call you?*) Take responsibility for helping in a way that can really be beneficial, perhaps long after everyone has left and the reality of the loss takes over.

- **Just think of all the years you had together and be grateful for them.** (*That's exactly what I'm thinking, and now I am all alone.*) Put yourself in the place of the bereaved. Would that statement make you feel better or worse?

- **Think of all of the reasons you still have to be happy.** (*Well, right now I can't get from the sad I am to the happy you want me to be.*) Grievers first need to move through this sad time before they can remember the cloud with the silver lining.

- **God wouldn't give you more than you can handle.** (*Gee, thanks, God.*) Does that mean that God let your child or your wife die just because you could handle it? Maybe in your view, God would do that, but others might not agree. Generally, it is best to keep your beliefs to yourself.

- **You can always get married again…** or **You're young; you can still have another child**. (*Let me never have to speak to this person ever again.*) These comments are so tactless and disdainful that they hardly bear explanation. NEVER make comments like this, even if that's what you think.

- **Now you can finally get on with your life.** (*What life?*) It takes time for the bereaved to move on. Grieving is part of "getting on with your life." Even if the relationship wasn't ideal, there can still be a feeling of loss for what could have been.

- **You had him for nine beautiful years.** (*But I won't have him for the next beautiful years – his birthdays, his graduation, his wedding, the birth of his first child, or the rest of my life.*) How would you feel if someone tried to tell you that about your own children?

- **It's been a year… it's time to get on with your life**. (*Let's see, how long did it take you to graduate from college? Get married? Go through that divorce? Get enough money to buy a house? Recover from your broken hip?*) Timetables are different for everyone. Who are we to judge each other?

We suggest to never start a sentence with the words "at least." Any time you say the words AT LEAST, you're going to make the recipient mad and close them off from anything else you say or do: "At least you had him for twenty-seven years" or "At least you have other children or can have more children" or "At least you can't see the scars" or "At least…"

What to Say to Those Who are Grieving

Listening and responding to the bereaved is often more important than any sympathetic statement or gesture you can make. Surprisingly few people actually take the time to listen, but being heard and understood is usually what the grieving person needs the most. Use the deceased's name when appropriate. Here are some phrases that seem to work well:

- I want to let you know that I was thinking of NAME today and that I know you still dearly miss him.
- I send you my love and kind thoughts.

- You are in my thoughts.

- I am including you in my prayers.

- My heart is aching for you.

- I don't know what to say. Please know that I am sorry for your loss.

- We love you…

- I still miss NAME…

- I am very sorry for your loss.

- You and NAME will be in my thoughts and prayers.

- My favorite memory of NAME is…

- We all need help at times like this; I am here for you.

- You can call me to share your sadness, day or late night.

We suggest that one of the best things to say is, "I would like to…" People in deep grief are often asked, "Is there anything we can do?" Take this one step further by offering to help with something specific, such as, "I'd like to take care of your snow shoveling this winter" or "I'd like to take you to the grocery store." Being specific makes it easier for the griever to take you up on your offer. Then follow through with a phone call, e-mail, or note. Include your contact information so the person, a friend, or a relative can contact you to schedule the task.

When visiting, if you don't know what to talk about, take the lead from the bereaved. Whether she wants to tell you about donating her husband's clothes to charity or taking up dance lessons, your main role is to be supportive. Words may be unimportant during times of profound grief. Respond emotionally. If it feels natural, do not hold back from clasping a hand with both of yours, placing a hand on the shoulder, or giving a heartfelt hug. When you hug, make it real – no "lite" hug gesture with a couple of "there, there" pats on the back.

You might decide to simply share some tears. Author and lecturer Leo Buscaglia often talked about a young boy whose next door neighbor was an elderly gentleman who had recently lost his wife. Upon seeing the man cry, the little boy went into the old gentleman's yard, climbed onto his lap, and just sat there. When his mother asked him what he had said to the neighbor, the little boy said, "Nothing, I just helped him cry."

There is a tendency for the bereaved to feel ashamed that they are still grieving, even months after the loss. She may report that she is doing "just fine" when, in reality, she just doesn't know how to handle the emptiness. Perhaps this is the best time to visit, take her on a shopping trip, bring over a meal to eat together, rake the leaves, dust, vacuum, or just sit and listen.

Appendix II
Websites with Related Resources

A web search using key words that relate to your situation will bring you a community of help, healing, caring, and comfort. The UK and Australia seem to have an abundance of great sites and organizations. Please send us links to additional sites, books and resources to add to our website and future editions of our book.

AGoodGoodbye.com – Gail Rubin is an expert and counselor in the area of how we look at and plan for our end. She has a book, *The Good Goodbye*, a blog called "The Family Plot," a web radio program, a Web TV program, and a DVD planning guide on how we look at death and the many alternatives in how we honor and celebrate our loved ones and ourselves.

ATimeToGrieve.org – From the UK, this site has a forum, a weekly online support group, and lots of links for those who have experienced a brain tumor journey.

CanadianVirtualHospice.ca – Provides support and personalized information about palliative and end-of-life care to patients, family members, healthcare providers, researchers, and educators.

CaringBridge.org – For families and friends experiencing a health event. The site allows family members to communicate information to a wide circle of people. Posted daily journal entries and the guestbook enable visitors to send the family messages of love and encouragement. The Support Planner section is a calendar that helps family and friends coordinate care and organize helpful tasks, like bringing a meal, offering rides, taking care of pets, and other needs.

CaringInfo.org – A program of the National Hospice and Palliative Care Organization (NHPCO) that has provided more than 1.3 million advance directives to individuals free of charge.

CenterForLoss.com – Dr. Alan Wolfelt has authored several books and presents at professional conferences around the world about supporting those in grief and loss and the importance of memorialization. He has many articles on his website and provides training for professionals.

ChildrenGrieve.org – The National Alliance for Grieving Children (NAGC) provides a network for nationwide communication between hundreds of professionals and volunteers who want to share ideas, information, and resources with each other to better support the grieving children and families they serve in their own communities.

Closure.org – An initiative to change expectations for end of life with easy-to-access, simple-to-understand information and resources to make educated decisions about end-of-life care.

CompassionAndSupport.org – Advance planning and care resources for families and professionals.

Creative-Funeral-Ideas.com – A resource for funerals, memorial services, or Celebrations of Life and ideas to help you cope with the funeral or memorial service planning.

Crossings.net – A home funeral and green burial resource center "to foster the integration of dying and after-death care back into our family and community life."

FinalFling.com – The UK's first one-stop shop for end-of-life planning that offers a free account with a set of planning tools that help sort your affairs so your family won't have to do it for you.

FuneralHelper.org – A wide range of useful information, including materials and suggestions for being an officiant and a list of helpful websites.

FuneralWise.com – Resources for preplanning a funeral for yourself, making funeral arrangements for a loved one, or providing grief support to a friend.

GoodLifeDeathGrief.org – UK information and resources from an alliance of organizations to raise awareness of ways of talking about and dealing with dying, death, and bereavement.

Grief.com – David Kessler has authored several books and speaks regularly at conferences around the country. Several articles and topical videos are on the site.

HealingTheSpirit.org – A large resource on grief and loss support and training for those connected to others who will are going through the grieving process. The site provides information about organ donation. There is also a place to post tributes for a lost loved one.

Heart2Soul.com – Resources to learn about funeral traditions and etiquette, including resources to help plan a funeral. A highly-respected group of experts provide the most comprehensive funeral information and experience on the web.

JourneyOfHearts.org – "A Healing Place in Cyberspace" for grief and loss information.

Legacy.com – List of grief support groups and advice on topics such as loss and grieving, sharing condolences, writing an obituary, and eulogy etiquette for funerals and memorial services.

MissFoundation.org/family/funeral.html – Support and resources after the death of a child, no matter their age or cause of death, as well as resources for professionals.

NatureDeath.org.uk – A long list of resources and links, especially for the UK. This site includes universal advice and links for other localities.

Recover-From-Grief.com – Resources about grief including loss of loved ones and pets.

MuchLoved.com – This site helps visitors create a tribute that includes pictures, words, and music. Family and friends can add their comments and pictures, too. The site is based in the UK, but contributors can be anywhere in the world. The site also includes information and support-sharing forums for grieving families and those planning for a loss.

SacredCrossings.com – A Los Angeles based company offering ministerial services, education, and guidance to families wishing to create green, cost-effective, and deeply meaningful funerals at home.

SevenPonds.com – Promotes a healthy attitude toward the process of death by encouraging a meaningful experience that is in harmony with the environment. It includes services / resources in the San Francisco Bay area.

YCollaborative.com – Houston, Texas, consultancy with a long list of links and lots of advice about making difficult, end-of-life decisions.

Related Books

Caring for Your Own Dead by Lisa Carlson. See UpperAccess.com/experts/carlson.html.

Caring for the Dead: Your Final Act of Love by Lisa Carlson. See UpperAccess.com/experts/carlson.html.

Can't We Talk About Something More Pleasant? by *New Yorker* magazine cartoonist Roz Chast. A funny, poignant, and graphic memoir of dealing with her parents in their seventies, eighties, and nineties. Book tour presentation on YouTube; NPR interview May 5, 2014, "All Things Considered"; RozChast.com.

Daddy, This is it - Being with my Dying Dad by Julie Saeger Nierenberg. This short book provides a model for what is possible in creating meaningful and heartfelt communications and closure at the end of life.

Final Rights: Reclaiming the American Way of Death by Lisa Carlson and Joshua Slocum. See UpperAccess.com/experts/carlson.html.

How to Plan a Celebration of Life Memorial Instead of a Funeral: A Practical, Step-by-Step Guide to Planning a Respectful and Loving Memorial Service by Norma Smith Davis.

I Died Laughing: Funeral Education with a Light Touch by Lisa Carlson. See UpperAccess.com/experts/carlson.html.

Knocking on Heaven's Door: The Path to a Better Way of Death by Katy Butler. This revolutionary blend of memoir and investigative reporting lays bare the tangled web of technology, medicine, and commerce that dying has become. The book also chronicles the rise of "Slow Medicine," a new movement trying to reclaim the "Good Deaths" our ancestors prized.

My Deepest Sympathies… Meaningful Sentiments for Condolence Notes and Conversations – Plus a Guide to Eulogies by Florence Isaacs.

No One Has to Die Alone – Preparing for a Meaningful Death by Lani Leary PhD. Leary has over twenty-five years of experience working with chronically ill, dying, and bereaved clients. Watch her Honolulu Ted talk video and buy her book if you are involved or will be involved in the dying of a friend or loved one. See DrLaniLeary.com.

Obit Kit, by Susan Soper, is a fill-in-the-blank workbook includes information on how you would like to be remembered – in your obituary and for generations to come. Visit ObitKit.com

Remembering Well: Rituals for Celebrating Life and Mourning Death by Sarah York. *Remembering Well* deals with complex and basic concerns related to bereavement. Sarah York explores issues, including violent deaths from murder or suicide, the deaths of children, organ donation, and family estrangement. At a basic level, she offers families, clergy, funeral professionals, and hospice workers guidelines for planning funerals and memorial services and understanding family dynamics around these issues. York is a retired Unitarian Universalist minister and author of several books. The 2nd edition is available from Amazon, Barnes & Noble, and Apollo Ranch Institute Press at ApolloRanchInstitutePress.com.

The Final Act of Living: Reflections of a Long-time Hospice Nurse Author Barbara Karnes has dedicated the last 32 years of her life to the education, care, and comforting of dying people and their loved ones, and the most useful things she's learned along the way have been distilled into her several books, booklets, and DVDs found at

BKBooks.com. See one of her presentations on our website (90 minutes).

The Party of Your Life: Get the Funeral You Want by Planning It Yourself by Erica Dillman. Gloomy funerals are out, and personalized life celebrations rule the day. Your memorial event can be a colorful, festive occasion; a simple, family-directed farewell in the comfort of your own home; or a weekend-long funeral palooza – any type of goodbye gala you want.

Tuesdays with Morrie by Mitch Albom. This book provides inspiration on how to live your life and the ending days of your life in a way that will be meaningful and heartfelt for you and the people with whom you share time.
MitchAlbom.com/d/film/3729/tuesdays-morrie

We Need to Talk about the Funeral: 101 Practical Ways to Commemorate and Celebrate a Life by Jane Morrell and Simon Smith. This book includes information on arranging a funeral, managing a relationship with a funeral director, and adding personal touches.

What to Say to a Friend Who's Sick by Letty Cottin Pogrebin. Letty became intrigued by the reactions of her family and friends after her diagnosis of breast cancer. Her book is about how to comfort, help, or even talk to patients without making them feel different or doomed.

See LettyCottinPogrebin.com and Amazon.com.

Videos

"Say Their Name" video (**Vimeo.com/69538289**) – The Compassionate Friends is a charitable organization of bereaved parents, siblings, and grandparents dedicated to supporting those who have suffered the death of a child. This film shares the feelings and experiences of parents' and siblings' grief to help others feel "normal" in their grief. The film also highlights the services offered by the charity to support the bereaved.

Online videos on **Ted.com** – "Ideas Worth Sharing":

- Judy MacDonald Johnston – "Prepare for a Good End of Life"
- Dr. Peter Saul – "Let's Talk about Dying"
- Dr. Lani Leary – "No One Has to Die Alone"

On **YouTube.com**:

- "My Last Days" is a series of inspiring profile videos about families with a member whose life is shortened by illness. Each of the 10 videos in the series shows how the families are inspired by the positive outlook of

the terminal loved one. Search for "My Last Days" on
SoulPancake.com.

- "The Last Chapter: End of Life Decisions" – West
  Virginia Public Broadcasting. Individuals battling end-
  stage disease reflect on how they want to live their final
  weeks. The one-hour program examines end-of-life
  care options and the need for advance directives,
  including a living will, a medical power of attorney,
  and a POST form (Physician Orders for Scope of
  Treatment). "The Last Chapter" also focuses on
  empowering individuals in having the last word on how
  they live at the end of their lives.

There is a continuously updated collection of related videos at
HeartfeltMemorialServices.com, so check back often.

From the Authors

Beverly Molander

As an ordained minister with an international organization, Centers for Spiritual Living, I am also a funeral officiant who has led and participated in many memorial celebrations, services, and ceremonies. I have noticed the challenges faced by those who find themselves responsible for planning and carrying out these important gatherings. While many of us are eager to embrace new ideas about how we can live life more fully, we get stumped when it comes to planning a fulfilling funeral or memorial service for someone we love. While many of us find comfort in the older traditions around death and dying, many would like to honor their loved one in alternative ways. After seeing so many people struggle around this issue, Dave Savage and I decided to create a book that offers a different perspective.

As a Baby Boomer among those born between 1946 and 1964, I have been a part of the generation that has shifted the outlook and attitude about every decade of life. It began with the "Make Love, Not War" slogan during the Vietnam era. We took a new road — moving more, divorcing more, having fewer kids and having them later in life, and tending toward philosophies that were more spiritual or secular than religious.

Today, members of my generation are losing parents and are entering the fall and winter of their own years. As we do, we are redefining the way we look at life and death. It seems only natural that those of us with an eclectic spiritual history would want to do something a little different from the traditional funeral and memorial services of the past.

With a background that includes Catholic, Southern Baptist, Unitarian Universalist, and Centers for Spiritual Living, I have found positive aspects from many religious and faith traditions. Although this book is for everyone, regardless of religious affiliation or tradition, we made the decision to include certain topics, such as readings and music, for people who have been previously disenfranchised and find those traditional religious services unappealing.

While we were writing *Heartfelt Memorial Services*, we realized that we were writing more about honoring relationships than simply planning a memorable event. Relationships don't begin or end with a memorial service. The loved one can be honored and appreciated long before and long after the actual death.

Dave Savage

I come from an extended family that excels at and takes great pleasure in marking life-cycle events in meaningful and creative ways. My parents, along with extended family and friends, were and are wordsmiths and excellent life-event organizers. My own memories of the ceremonies they created for our family have helped to shape our book.

I was brought up in a loving home that could be religiously described as Jewish Humanist. In holiday celebrations, "God" references were generally left out in favor of references to family values and connection.

For more than twelve years, I was affiliated with the Society for Humanistic Judaism (SHJ.org) and led a Jewish holiday celebration group for adults and families. We offered a culture-centered approach to Judaism. Many mixed-faith families attended, which led to a further use of inclusive and welcoming language for the many holiday and life-cycle services and ceremonies I created.

I was also active in a Unitarian Universalist congregation for more than twenty-five years, creating and participating in all kinds of services and ceremonies. This afforded me the opportunity to witness a variety of end-of-life markers and celebrations and expand my awareness of the importance of these events.

As owner of Memory Keepers Video, I have recorded many kinds of religious and life-cycle gatherings, including memorial services and funerals. I encourage families and friends to use those special times before and after an event to share and record their treasured memories and family histories.

As a volunteer at a local hospice, I organize gatherings to record individuals and families as they share memories and messages with those they love. These will be passed on as part of a rich and heartfelt family legacy. Perhaps an even more personal reason for writing this book is to help me prepare for the services I will need to arrange for my parents, who are currently in their 80s. They continue to be great role models for me, and I want to find ways to honor them before and after their passing. At the same time, I am recording my own preferences for those who will one day be planning ceremonies for me.

Final Thoughts

Thank you for reading our book. Additional and updated materials can be found at our website HeartfeltMemorialServices.com.

We also provide:

- consulting, planning, and officiating for families
- workshops and presentations for companies, organizations, and conferences
- custom and private label editions of our book and materials (currently used for marketing, training, and complimentary gifts for clients, students and volunteers)

We look forward to learning how our materials made a difference for your family, friends, clients, patients, or residents. Please contact us with any questions, or to give a review of the book. We would appreciate learning how our advice or materials benefited your family or friends.

Thank you,
Dave and Beverly

Notes

Made in the USA
Las Vegas, NV
23 June 2024

91382627R00148